40 Ways to Get Closer to God

40 Ways to
Get Closer to God

JERRY MACGREGOR
WITH KERI WYATT KENT

BETHANY HOUSE PUBLISHERS

a division of Baker Publishing Group
Minneapolis, Minnesota

© 2011 by Jerry MacGregor

Written with Keri Wyatt Kent

Published by Bethany House Publishers
11400 Hampshire Avenue South
Bloomington, Minnesota 55438
www.bethanyhouse.com

Bethany House Publishers is a division of
Baker Publishing Group, Grand Rapids, Michigan

Printed in the United States of America

All rights reserved. No part of this publication may be reproduced, stored in a retrieval system,
or transmitted in any form or by any means—electronic, mechanical, photocopying, recording,
or otherwise—without the prior written permission of the publisher. The only exception is brief
quotations in printed reviews.

                    Library of Congress Cataloging-in-Publication Data
MacGregor, Jerry.
      40 ways to get closer to God / Jerry MacGregor with Keri Wyatt Kent.
          p.   cm.
      Summary: "Forty days of practical exercises for Christians to enhance their love of God
   and put their faith into action"—Provided by publisher.
      Includes bibliographical references.
      ISBN 978-0-7642-0918-5 (pbk. : alk. paper)
      1. Spiritual life—Christianity. I. Kent, Keri Wyatt. II. Title. III. Title: Forty ways to get
   closer to God.
   BV4501.3.M2335 2011
   248—dc23   2011025208

Unless otherwise identified, Scripture quotations are from the Holy Bible, New International Version. NIV Copyright © 1973, 1978, 1984, 2011 by Biblica, Inc. Used by permission of Zondervan.
All rights reserved worldwide. www.zondervan.com.

Scripture quotations identified NASB are from the New American Standard Bible, copyright
© 1960, 1962, 1963, 1968, 1971, 1972, 1973, 1975, 1977, 1995 by The Lockman Foundation.
Used by permission.

Scripture quotations identified NLT are from the Holy Bible, New Living Translation, copyright
© 1996, 2004, 2007 by Tyndale House Foundation. Used by permission of Tyndale House Publishers, Inc., Carol Stream, Illinois 60188. All rights reserved.

Scripture quotations identified NRSV are from the New Revised Standard Version of the Bible,
copyright © 1989, by the Division of Christian Education of the National Council of the Churches
of Christ in the United States of America. Used by permission. All
rights reserved.

Scripture quotations identified KJV are from the King James Version of the Bible.

The internet addresses, email addresses, and phone numbers in this
book are accurate at the time of publication. They are provided as a
resource. Baker Publishing Group does not endorse them or vouch
for their content or permanence.

Cover design by Jeff Miller/Faceout Studio

Author is represented by MacGregor Literary.

In keeping with biblical principles of
creation stewardship, Baker Publishing Group advocates the responsible
use of our natural resources. As a
member of the Green Press Initiative, our company uses recycled
paper when possible. The text paper
of this book is composed in part of
post-consumer waste.

*This book is for Colin, Holly, and Maelie—
may you grow close to God as you see Him
at work in your life together.*

The God Challenge

Would you like to move closer to God? If so, let's get one thing straight right off the bat—I'm no shining example. I didn't write this book because I am perfect or have it all figured out. I don't glow in the dark. I wrote it because, well, I'm a wreck. I want to be a better Christian. I want to feel really close to God, but I can't seem to ever quite get there. I sin, ask forgiveness, and sin again. I don't have all the answers, and I don't want you to think, *This guy wrote a book because he really has it all together.* I don't.

But I'm fifty-two while writing this sentence, and looking back over the past forty years, I realize I've come a ways in my walk with God. I used to be farther away, and now I'm closer. Most of that is because of *books* and *people*—books that have shared good ideas with me for how I could move forward in my spiritual walk, and people who have helped me actually put those ideas into practice. So I wrote this book as a "God challenge." In other words, I thought I could create something that would challenge you, ask you to try some ideas and to do some work, with the end result being that you'll have moved a bit further down the path in your spiritual walk.

In this book you'll find a bunch of spiritual practices I've tried and used and found to be effective. There's nothing phony in here—none of that dopey, made-up-for-a-book, try-this-even-though-I-never-have sort of thing. Everything here is practical and real. In fact, if you ran into me somewhere and we started talking about how to grow close to God, these are the very ideas I'd share with you from my own experience.

And listen: There's no shortcut. Just reading this book won't make you more spiritual, in the same way that watching Peyton Manning on TV won't make you a great quarterback. It takes work to get better at anything. Nobody buys a guitar one day and starts selling concert tickets the next. You don't pick up a set of golf clubs on Wednesday and expect to win the tournament on Saturday. If you're serious about it, you do some work. You try it out. You practice. You start with the basics, learn them, and then keep practicing until you get better. In time, you notice improvement—whether it's golf or music or cooking or growing up in Jesus. Real spiritual growth takes time and effort.

So this book is a place to start. You read it, try it out, and see what happens. Maybe you talk about the ideas with a couple of friends, and you decide to try these ideas together.

Or maybe you take a solitary approach and decide to write your thoughts down so they're on paper and available for later reflection. Journaling is a great way to dig into those thoughts. Use the writing spaces provided and explore what you're thinking and feeling. Writing down our concerns and struggles validates their place in our lives. There's no hiding when we write our thoughts down.

· Don't expect miracles here, 'cause I'm fresh out. What I can promise you is this: *Disciplines are the ONLY strategy I know for growing your Christian life.* I figure you've purchased this book because those other methods you tried (going to Sunday school, tithing, praying before meals, watching televangelists) were nice but didn't really help you go deep with God.

Those practices aren't bad, of course. They just don't go far enough. So instead, I'm offering you a realistic plan to get closer to God. Try this book for forty days. Do the exercises, and see if you're not further down the path when you're done. At the end, you should have some fundamental skills for moving forward, for growing deeper, for drawing closer to God.

If you too are a wreck, my prayer for you is that you'll discover you have much greater spiritual depth than you thought when you began this book. I wish you all the best as you start walking the path.

JERRY MacGREGOR
NEHALEM, OREGON

DAY ONE

At Your Service

The primary reason Jesus calls us to servanthood is not just because other people need our service. It is because of what happens to us when we serve.[1]

—JOHN ORTBERG

If you ask most people to tell you about a time when they felt truly fulfilled, odds are they will not tell you a story about a time when they focused on their own needs and wants. Rather, they will likely recall an incident where they set their own agenda aside and helped someone else. Maybe they tutored an inner-city kid or went on a mission trip or served Christmas dinner at a soup kitchen. Perhaps they performed some simple act of service for their own family, or assisted a neighbor or close friend. The practice of serving others actually brings us joy, if we undertake it with the right attitude.

Despite the fact that serving others often brings us fulfillment, many people don't do it. We have great intentions, but we're *so busy.* And besides, how do you know which needs, of the many around you, to address?

I think many of us spend more energy than we realize keeping ourselves isolated from the needs of others. We may not be aware that right in our backyard (as Mother Teresa would say), there is a Calcutta. Our neighbors may not be starving or have leprosy, but they can be suffering or hurting in some way, and it's possible we could do something simple to show love to them.

It's human nature to be self-focused. That's why Jesus had to teach his followers to be unselfish. He had to instruct them on servanthood, because it doesn't come naturally. He told his followers: "If anyone would come after me, he must deny himself and take up his cross and follow me. For whoever wants to save his life will lose it, but whoever loses his life for me and for the gospel will save it" (Mark 8:34–35).

He also said, "Whoever wants to become great among you must be your servant, and whoever wants to be first must be slave of all. For even the Son of Man did not come to be served, but to serve, and to give his life as a ransom for many" (Mark 10:43–45).

When we let go of our agenda and focus on serving others, we "save" our own lives. When we serve others, we experience God's love and true fulfillment. And those we serve get a tangible experience of his love through us. Who wouldn't find that exhilarating? I believe most of us know that, deep down. But it's still difficult to embrace the spiritual practice of service—to actually get out and *do* something. Sure, we think it would be nice to be a do-gooder. We think volunteerism is noble. But again, we're busy, or we don't know what to do, or maybe we don't feel like serving anyone. It's inconvenient to do so. It takes time we think we don't have.

And yet, if we claim to be followers of Jesus, service is exactly what we are called to do. Jesus said that if we want to get ahead in his kingdom we have to love others by serving them. And he didn't offer a plan B. Serving teaches you things you can't learn any other way. Serving teaches you humility in a way that talking about humility never will. *It allows you to actually imitate Christ, which is the goal of the Christian faith.*

Look, sometimes we have to be obedient, even if it is tough. We have to decide to love, because servanthood is an expression of our love for God, and our love for others. So the point of service is to love others tangibly.

Too many Christians get confused and think the goal of our faith is to be fulfilled or to realize our potential. Um . . . that's not what Christ said. The goal of our faith is to become more like Jesus, to act as he would if he were living in our place. Serving others leads to Christlikeness.

🌱 TODAY'S CHALLENGE

Your challenge today is to serve someone in a practical way. The first step is to find someone in need of service. Unfortunately, many of us live our lives isolated from need (or we simply ignore it when it's right under our noses). But most church bulletins list people who are in need of prayer for one reason or another—sickness, unemployment, a death in the family. This week, find someone from your church or your neighborhood who is going through a difficult time. You may have to ask your pastor to recommend someone if your church doesn't share such information publicly.

Perhaps a friend can tell you about a single mom or a family with a chronically ill child, or someone who needs to have God's love shown to them in very tangible and practical ways.

Your job: Write a note of encouragement to the person you've decided to help. Deliver the note along with some practical help. You may decide to make a meal (or buy one, if you cook like me) and bring it to the family. I've discovered you can pick up a frozen lasagna, a bagged salad, and a loaf of pre-made garlic bread, and you've got a "homemade" meal to share. Or just deliver a bag of groceries with some basics—bread, milk, eggs, canned soup, peanut butter, and jelly.

Of course, you may decide to provide other forms of help: mowing a lawn, shoveling snow, doing simple home repairs. Make yourself available and listen to what someone needs, then simply meet that need.

Right now, you may be thinking, *Holy cow! Is THAT what this book is going to demand of me? That I actually go and DO something?* Well . . . yes. Sorry, but there's no shortcut to spiritual growth. If you really want to get closer to God, you're going to have to break out of your old patterns, step out in faith, and try something new. So I started you out with a task that may make you uncomfortable . . . but it's a task you *can* do. All of us are able to do some simple act of service for someone else in need. So get out of that chair and go serve somebody.

____ *Check here when you have completed today's God Challenge.*

Notes

Hungry for God

We are beginning to realize that we hunger for God and
that for far too long we have settled for far too little.[2]

—JOHN KIRVAN

Every year, Americans spend an estimated $40 to $50 billion
trying to lose weight—buying diet books, signing up for Jenny
Craig, joining Weight Watchers, and working with others who
provide meals, support, and counseling, for a price. They all
offer generally the same advice: Eat less, move more. Still, the
diet industry continues to grow.

Yet every year obesity rates climb. And the percentage of
Americans who are morbidly obese rises as well. Something is
wrong with this picture.

Why is this? Perhaps it has something to do with the fact that
from the time we are very young, our culture has been shaping
us. That culture tells us to indulge. It refers to people as "consum-
ers." We are constantly told not just that we ought to buy, eat, or
drink, but that doing so will somehow make us happy, successful,

and popular. Most of us believe that if we can afford to indulge our appetites, we have the right to do so. We "deserve" a steak dinner or a triple hot fudge sundae.

An important step of growth toward God is to realize that our culture is not "normal." We are far more focused on consumption and acquisition than most of the world. So the first step toward healing is to gain an accurate view of ourselves. We need to realize that some of our indulgences are not freedom, but the prison of addiction.

For centuries, in many cultures around the world, an important spiritual practice was that of fasting—giving up food (or other things we enjoy) for a certain amount of time in order to focus on God and pray. It is still common in many parts of the world.

In our culture, fasting is not popular, but it is perhaps necessary for spiritual growth. Fasting can take many forms. For some, an appetite for *things* is far greater than the appetite for *food*. Fasting from the Internet, for example, even for a day, might be harder (and more spiritually healthy) than simply abstaining from food. *So don't think of fasting as merely skipping a meal, but as putting off something we enjoy doing in order to focus on God.*

When Jesus taught about fasting, he began by saying, "When you fast . . ." He didn't say, "*If* you fast . . ." Fasting was a normal part of religious life for Jews in his culture.

Why would we even want to deny ourselves in this way? Obviously, we can pray without fasting, so why bother?

Marjorie Thompson, in her book *Soul Feast,* writes:

In the ancient Jewish tradition, fasting had two primary purposes. The first was to express personal or national repentance for sin.

The second purpose was to prepare oneself inwardly for receiving the necessary strength and grace to complete a mission of faithful service in God's name.[3]

Perhaps the reason we don't fast is that we really don't do much repenting. We take grace for granted and label our sins as "youthful indiscretion" or simply "mistakes." We're also a bit weak on the concept of mission—we grind through life and do not see the challenges in our way as a God-given mission. We substitute watching others engage in battle (in sports) or adventure (action movies or video games) and never consider the possibility that perhaps God has a real adventure he wants us to embark upon.

Fasting can take us deeper into our spiritual lives and provide clarity about what really matters, what really feeds our souls.

As Thompson observes,

Are we aware of how much sustains our life apart from physical food? Do we have an inner conviction that *Christ* is our life? We will comprehend little of how we are nourished by Christ until we have emptied ourselves of the kinds of sustenance that keep us content to live at life's surface.[4]

Does that describe you? "Content to live at life's surface"? Or perhaps you are anything but content—you want to live a life that is deeper and richer. You are hungry for God.

Ironically, the practice of fasting can begin to satisfy that hunger. It is not an easy practice, but it is one you can slowly get better at. If you've ever tried to change your lifestyle, for example, by exercising, you know you can't just jump off the couch and run a marathon. Fasting, similarly, is a practice best begun in small steps.

The Bible is very clear that fasting is a practice that is to be combined with prayer. The idea is to voluntarily abstain from food or from something else in order to focus on God and be "fed" by his Word and by prayer.

🌳 Today's Challenge

Today, your challenge is to try a very simple form of fasting. Instead of eating lunch during your lunch break, spend the time reading a couple of psalms, then take a bit of time for prayer. Perhaps you will want to focus your prayers on a specific situation you're facing where you feel you need God's help. Perhaps you will intercede on behalf of a friend or family member who is sick or facing some sort of struggle. (*Note:* Loading up on a huge breakfast because you know you will miss the noon meal will backfire, trust me; so eat normally at breakfast and dinner.)

Jesus said that when we fast we're not to make a big deal of it (see Matthew 6:16–18). So during your normal lunch break, get alone. If someone asks you to lunch, tell them you have an appointment. (You don't have to tell them it's with God.) Spend your time praying instead of eating.

In the afternoon, you may feel a bit hungry. Resist the urge to snack—wait until dinner. Drink water. Let hunger pains remind you of God's presence with you, and remind you to pray, even in the midst of your daily activities. Allow his love to sustain you.

I can tell you that fasting has been one of the most significant practices to enhance my spiritual life. I've fasted from food (as well as from TV, the news, Facebook, the Web, and sports at various times) in order to focus on God, and I have always found that it helps me to grow in my spiritual walk. Give it a try today.

_____ *Check here when you have completed today's God Challenge.*

Notes

DAY THREE

Make It Stick

What the mind repeats, it retains.[5]

—JOHN ORTBERG

My friend Kaye is an upbeat, beautiful woman with a great smile. However, she lives a challenging life. She's afflicted with Parkinson's disease, multiple sclerosis, and heart disease, to name only a few of her long list of ailments. She's had surgeries, hospital stays, and pain. Sometimes the doctors aren't sure what causes her symptoms, other times they are completely sure, but the prognosis is often painful.

But Kaye is one of the most positive people I know. When you ask her why, she replies that it's because of God. You get the idea that Kaye has an intimacy with God few people experience. Often when people face chronic illness, they spend a lot of time asking why, raging at God. But Kaye's struggles have pushed her straight into God's arms. It's not that she hasn't questioned him, but rather *that she has somehow heard a reply that has given her peace.* She's chosen to deal with her problems by turning to Scripture. Kaye doesn't just read it; she makes it stick.

Over the years, Kaye has memorized more than five hundred Bible verses. She laughed a bit self-consciously when she told me her favorite method of memorizing: She'll set the words of Scripture to the tune of one of the rock 'n' roll "oldies" she enjoys. She'll read a passage and realize it fits into the cadence of a familiar song, then sing it all day until she has the words memorized.

One day, Kaye was in the hospital recovering from one of her many surgeries. Her arms were too weak to even hold her Bible, and she started to feel sorry for herself because she couldn't do the one thing that would bring her comfort—read her Bible. But then God gently reminded her that she didn't need to read . . . she could simply remember. So in that hospital bed, she began to "read" what was in her heart. She kept at it for more than an hour, singing and reciting God's Word.

Like most people who have memorized Scripture, Kaye finds that God will bring the right verses to mind at the right time to give her peace, guidance, or advice about a specific situation. Many of us wish that God would do this for us—give us directions along the way in our spiritual journey.

Here's an important truth: *God will not bring the words of Scripture to our minds unless we stash those words in our hearts first.* When we deposit the truths of Scripture into our lives, we have something to draw on in times of trouble. Then, when we are intimately familiar with God's voice, we will recognize it. I believe that for many people, God may very well be speaking, but they remain deaf to his gentle whispers because they haven't spent the time to recognize his voice. What God impresses on our spirits will not contradict what he says in Scripture. But if we are unacquainted with his voice, we will not be able to pick it out amid the din of other voices competing for our attention.

Memorizing Scripture is a hedge against sin, as Psalm 119 points out. God can use it to convict of the truth. It also shapes our prayers. We can take the words of Scripture and pray them back to God. If you aren't a part of a liturgical tradition, praying words someone else has written may feel awkward at first. You may think it's more authentic to ad-lib your prayers, to pray what's in your heart. But written prayers can be a helpful tool for spiritual growth.

Walter Wangerin writes:

> We are surrounded by a host of those whose grace it is to pray well! Psalmists, poets, martyrs, saints and witnesses, men and women of gentle faith, people of suffering and of joy. And what shall we do with their gifts? It is no less a prayer if we take their words and make them our own, for one may build a beautiful house and then give it away so that another one might live in it.[6]

How much easier to pray the Psalms if we have a few memorized. And memorizing is not really difficult—you've memorized hundreds of things, from advertising jingles to telephone numbers to top-40 hits. I was in my car singing along with the radio recently and realized I probably have hundreds of songs stored in my memory bank. As a teenager, you might have had dozens of lines from movies committed to memory. I spent years doing theater, and memorized countless lines of dialogue. The challenge is to take that skill and apply it to learning God's Word.

🌱 TODAY'S CHALLENGE

One more thing about my friend Kaye: When you talk to her about the Bible, you realize pretty quickly that she loves God's

Word. So she's motivated by love. I think that's an important starting point.

Some of the easiest Scripture to memorize is the Psalms. These are prayers in poetic form, making them easy to sing or recite. So today, your challenge is to memorize Psalm 121, a familiar and well-loved psalm. By placing these words in your heart, you will equip yourself to face challenges. You will affirm the truth that God has your back—that he is vigilant in protecting you and always aware of the challenges you face. You'll find these words coming to mind at precisely the right time.

Experiment with different memorization methods to see what works for you. Try reading the words out loud, slowly, several times. Read one verse; then try to say it without reading it. Keep repeating it. Try copying it down several times, and then writing it without copying. My favorite method is to copy the passage onto a note card or two. When I have a few minutes during the day, I flip through the cards. I put the reference on one side, the words on the other, and practice until I can say all the words just by looking at the reference. Perhaps you'll want to try Kaye's method of putting the words to a familiar tune. Psalm 121 has been turned into a worship chorus more than once, so perhaps the first few verses will be familiar to you because of that.

Here are the words from the NIV translation. If you like, read the verse in several different translations to see which one you'd prefer to commit to memory.

PSALM 121

I lift up my eyes to the hills—
where does my help come from?

My help comes from the Lord,
  the Maker of heaven and earth.

He will not let your foot slip—
  he who watches over you will not slumber;

indeed, he who watches over Israel
  will neither slumber nor sleep.

The Lord watches over you—
  the Lord is your shade at your right hand;

the sun will not harm you by day,
  nor the moon by night.

The Lord will keep you from all harm—
  he will watch over your life;

the Lord will watch over your coming and going
  both now and forevermore.

_____ Check here when you have completed today's God Challenge.

Notes

....

....

....

....

....

....

....

Write It Down

I never lost the ability to write. In fact, writing became part of my struggle for survival. It gave me the little distance from myself that I needed to keep from drowning in my despair.[7]

—Henri Nouwen

When we want to remember something, we record it. Whether it's on a Post-it note, legal tablet, leather-bound journal, photograph, videotape, or online journal doesn't matter, as long as the item is safely backed up.

Proverbs 7:1–3 tells us we must remember what we have been taught, that our very life depends on that material being written on our hearts. "Keep my commands and you will live; guard my teachings as the apple of your eye. Bind them on your fingers; write them on the tablet of your heart." Journaling reinforces for our minds what we believe in our hearts, and for the Christian, this is an excellent exercise. As we take these challenges to heart and seek God in fresh new ways, keeping a journal can help us stay the course. At the end of each day's challenge is a space for your thoughts and perceptions.

Writing can be a huge help to our journey as Christians. During the high points and while we steadfastly push through the lows, putting our thoughts down on paper has a way of renewing our focus. Consider some of these journal keepers and why they filled up the white spaces of their journals with the scribbles of their hearts:

> Keep a notebook or journal of lessons learned. This is not a diary of events, but a record of what you are learning. Write down the insights and life lessons God teaches you about him, about yourself, about life, relationships, and everything else. . . . The reason we must relearn lessons is that we forget them. Reviewing your spiritual journal regularly can spare you a lot of unnecessary pain and heartache.[8]
>
> RICK WARREN

> Why do we do it, we writers? "Of making many books there is no end," sighed the Teacher of Ecclesiastes. . . . I think we do it because each of us has nothing else to offer than a living point of view that differentiates us from every other person on this planet. We must tell our stories to someone.[9]
>
> PHILIP YANCEY

> On the pages of a journal, in the privacy of a moment, we can take tentative steps into truth and scour our feelings.[10]
>
> ADELE CALHOUN

There's no prize for perfect essays or even great handwriting, and no two people will have the same journal, which is actually a very freeing notion. Often people shy away from journaling because of what they envision it should look like. But a journal is simply a place to write down what you feel, think, believe, question, and accept. Don't worry about length, indenting, or whether you should have used a list instead of a paragraph. It could be a letter never to be sent, a heartfelt re-rendering of a psalm, a prayer request, or praise. The important thing is to record your perceptions and to take inventory of your thoughts.

TODAY'S CHALLENGE

Start today. Find a pen, decide what it is you want to remember, and place those thoughts captive on the page.

_____ *Check here when you have completed today's God Challenge.*

Notes

What's Love Got to Do With It?

Only Christianity dares to make God's love unconditional.[11]

—Philip Yancey

In his book *What's So Amazing About Grace?* Philip Yancey points out that the Bible is unique among the holy books of major world religions because it is the only one that describes God as loving us unconditionally. In fact, it goes even further and declares, "God *is* love."

Christian theology is unique because of the doctrine of grace. God, according to the Bible, is not only good and just and holy, but slow to anger and abounding in love. That love is not based on our performance or goodness, but is completely unconditional.

The word *love*, in our culture, is overused. The phrase "I love you, man" drips with irony and sarcasm, thanks to beer commercials and a movie of the same title.

The New Testament was written in Greek, which had three words translated *love*: *phileo,* which means to feel or show brotherly love or affection; *eros,* which is sensual or erotic love (a word not found in the New Testament); and *agapao,* which means to love with deep, self-sacrificing love—the way that God loves us, and that we ought to love one another.

God truly does love human beings in this way. He created them and sacrificed himself for them. But what does that mean? Because the word *love* has lost so much of its meaning today, it's easy to skip over this amazing truth—God truly loves you. It's easy to talk about God loving human beings in general, but have you ever really thought about the fact that God earnestly cares for you, specifically? That he loves you personally?

God offers a love that's in spite of your mistakes, not because of your accomplishments. His love has absolutely no strings attached. It is the one thing in this life that sounds too good to be true, but actually *is* true. You not only don't have to earn it, you *can't* earn it. Our attempts to impress him simply will not work. That's not because he's ambivalent, but because he already loves you so completely that nothing you do could make him love you any more than he already does.

Where else in this world will you find that? Nowhere. At work you have to continually impress your boss, improve your performance, and inspire your employees to keep your job. At home perhaps you get a little more grace than at work, but in general, your spouse and kids are probably not as patient with you as God is. They expect you to behave decently. Your friends may put up with a lot, but they will let you down once in a while, because they are human.

Yet God loves us through all our failures, bad choices, and mistakes. It's not that he ignores our sin—but he *is* love. And he wants us to love him back. He wants us to respond to his love by loving him and others. We often fail at that, and he gives us another chance. His mercies really are new every morning.

In his book *Crazy Love*, pastor and author Francis Chan says that we would love God more if we fully understood his infinite love for us. He writes: "It confuses us when loving God is hard. Shouldn't it be easy to love a God so wonderful? When we love God because we feel we *should* love Him, instead of genuinely loving out of our true selves, we have forgotten who God really is." [12]

Jesus came to show us what God's love looks like, who God really is. And he also told us what our response to that love should be. He said the two most important commandments were to "love the Lord your God with all your heart, soul, mind and strength, and to love your neighbor as yourself." That's how we are to respond to God's love. But it's not easy to respond to something until you understand it. So rather than powering up and trying to be more loving, perhaps the best way to love God and love people is to take a good look at God's love. If we have forgotten who God is, reading his Word will help us to remember.

🌳 Today's Challenge

Nothing connects us with God's love like reading through some of the countless verses of Scripture that focus on that amazing love. Today, your challenge is to study God's love. Specifically, you are going to do a word study on the word *love*.

Get yourself a concordance (most Bibles have one in the appendix, or you can get one at a Christian bookstore—or use an online Bible site like *www.biblegateway.com*). Do a search on all the verses that contain the word *love*. Take your time reading through as many verses as you can—you won't get through all of them, and that's okay. In the journaling space below, write down a few verses that are especially meaningful to you, plus any insights that come as a result of your study. That's all. Just see the richness that Scripture brings to something as simple as looking at an important word of faith.

After you spend some time studying the word *love*, pray—and thank God for his love for you.

___ *Check here when you have completed today's God Challenge.*

Notes

Pray Constantly

How we spend our days is, of course, how we spend our lives. [13]

—Annie Dillard

For millennia, the people of God have sought him in prayer. Not only in moments of need, but in a scheduled sort of way. Whether it is a weekly prayer meeting, a daily quiet time, or short prayers throughout the day, a rhythm of prayer helps keep us on track.

Jesus grew up following the Jewish custom of praying this prayer twice a day: "Hear, O Israel: The Lord our God, the Lord is one" (Deuteronomy 6:4). It was known as the *Shema,* and was followed in the morning by other prayers straight from the pages of the Torah (our Old Testament), and in the evening by personal petitions.

Author and pastor Adele Calhoun writes: "After Jesus' death, his disciples continued to pray at fixed hours of the day (Acts 3:1; 10:3, 9, 30). This custom of praying at set daily intervals quickly became part of the early church's rhythm of prayer." [14]

Some traditions continued what is known as the liturgy of the hours, or the daily office, using set prayers for certain times of the day. Robert Benson writes, "For thousands of years, the daily office has been a primary way to hold ourselves in closer communion with the One who made us. It is a way to sanctify our days and our hours, our work and our love, our very life itself."[15]

It may seem daunting to pray at regular intervals, especially every hour. However, too often we intend to pray but make no actual *plans* to do so. Intention will get you nowhere without decision. *So if you're going to get close to God, you've got to decide to pray regularly.*

While any practice has the potential to become legalistic, it also has the potential to be a life-giving support structure. Praying at regular intervals reminds us to stop, to breathe, to recalibrate our minds so that we are not focused only on ourselves, our work, and our worries. It gives us the opportunity to give those things to God and to pray for those around us.

The practice of praying several times each day is actually related to the practice of slowing—living at a pace that doesn't exhaust us. The purpose of praying at set times through the day is not to be able to check it off our list or say that we did it. *We are not earning God's approval, but attuning ourselves to his rhythm.* We are slowing down enough to notice the work of God all around us. We are taking the time to refuel our souls.

The apostle Paul wrote to a young church: "Rejoice always, pray continually, give thanks in all circumstances; for this is God's will for you in Christ Jesus" (1 Thessalonians 5:16–18). Why did he give them this advice? Because to rejoice, pray, and give thanks is a choice. If we only rejoice when things go exceptionally well, if we only pray when we need something, we turn God into a cosmic vending machine. When we choose to make rejoicing, prayer, and gratitude a part of each hour of our day, we are transformed.

We should remember that although it is helpful to talk to God, prayer is much broader than simply "saying prayers." Prayer is also about listening to God, whether he speaks through the Bible, other people, or gentle impressions in our own spirit. To pray constantly is to cultivate an attitude of prayerful attention. What if praying continually means keeping an ear open to the whispers of God? Wouldn't continual listening for God's whispers be continuous prayer too?

🌱 TODAY'S CHALLENGE

You may want to explore the seven prayers that are included in the traditional "daily office" created by St. Benedict in AD 600. Several Web sites have readings for morning and evening prayers. You can find them listed on *www.dailyoffice.org* or *www.commonprayer.org*.

But for today, *your challenge is to simply turn your mind toward God throughout the day.* This is a way to put 1 Thessalonians 5:17 into practice. You are going to pray once an hour, but only for a few minutes. Hopefully this will help you get into a habit of talking to God and listening to him throughout your day.

Imagine what your day would look like if you knew you would never have to face any challenge, no matter how great, by yourself. When facing a decision at work, you'd immediately talk to God about it. When something good happened, whether with a friend, your spouse, or your kids, you'd reflexively say, "Thanks, God." Today's challenge is the first step in building that kind of habit in your heart.

Set a timer on your phone, PDA, or watch to go off once an hour. When you hear the beep, simply stop for a moment and take a deep breath. Give whatever it is you are working on at that moment to God. If you are in the midst of a conversation, silently invite God into it, asking for his wisdom and love to pervade the interaction. Even if you are watching television or reading, take a minute to assess what's going on in your heart. How do you feel about what you're watching or reading, knowing God is present with you? Are you content? Dissatisfied? Angry? Joyful? Embarrassed by his presence? Talk to God about it—even though nothing you tell him will surprise him, he still loves to hear from you. If you happen to be talking with a stranger (maybe the person behind the counter at the bank or a fast-food restaurant), ask how you could pray for them.

Getting started with a regular prayer habit will change your life like nothing you've done before.

_____ *Check here when you have completed today's God Challenge.*

Notes

Day Seven

Keep It Simple

Simplicity is an acquired taste. Mankind, left free, instinctively complicates life.

—Katherine F. Gerould

Do you ever find yourself lost in an escape fantasy? Ever find yourself thinking there has got to be more to life than this? That if you could just get out of the city/suburbs/country and move to the country/city/suburbs, you could live a simpler life?

The economic recession of the late 1980s prompted many so-called yuppies (young urban professionals) to cash out their 401(k)s and move to Vermont to open bed-and-breakfasts or start cheese farms. Subsequent economic downturns have inspired similar exoduses from the rat race. *But—changing locations won't change who you are.* Many found what Richard Carlson and Joseph Bailey observed was true: "You can rearrange the externals of your life in a radically different way, but you always take your thinking with you. If you are a hurried, rushed person in the city, you'll also be a hurried, rushed person in the country." [16]

Our culture values efficiency and speed: getting things done and moving fast. And yet we long for simplicity. Magazines, television shows, and books are dedicated to telling us how to simplify. We sometimes imagine that this desire for simplicity is due to the fast blur of our lives and the stress that seems so inescapable. It's because we live in the twenty-first century with its rapidly changing technology. To a degree, this is true. However, perhaps it has always been true. Read this description and see if it resonates:

> Our lives . . . grow too complex and overcrowded. Even the necessary obligations that we feel we must meet grow overnight, like Jack's beanstalk, and before we know it we are bowed down with burdens, crushed under committees, strained, breathless, and hurried, panting through a never-ending program of appointments. We are too busy. . . . We're weary and breathless. And we know and regret that our life is slipping away, with our having tasted so little of the peace and joy and serenity we are persuaded it should yield. . . . We feel honestly the pull of many obligations and try to fulfill them all.[17]

Does this sound like your life? These words were penned in 1941 by Thomas Kelly, who complained that the age of "radio and auto," more than half a century ago, had speeded up his life to one far faster-paced than his grandparents'. Don't you wonder what he would have thought of text messaging, e-mail, and Skype? Of people who use those technologies while driving a car seventy miles an hour on the freeway?

What does it mean to simplify? Is it about organizing our closets or desks? For years, Christians have practiced the discipline of simplicity, and it has little to do with living space or time management. Rather, *simplicity has to do with focus.*

Jesus said, "Seek first his kingdom and his righteousness, and all these things will be given to you as well." (See Matthew 6:33.) What things? Jesus had been teaching on how we shouldn't worry about food, clothing, shelter—the basic necessities of life that take up so much of our energy and time. Just focus on God, he said, and the rest will fall into place.

Simplicity, according to Jesus, is about having a singular focus on God. Our lives become simple when what we focus on, what we are seeking, is the kingdom of God.

Which is something we would all like to do, right? At least, mostly we would. But we get distracted. We lose our train of thought. So much competes for our attention that we forget about simplicity and fill our lives with complexities. Much of this comes to us via the channels we now call "the media." Media is the plural of medium—the way in which a message is conveyed. Artists work using different media—pottery, textiles, oil paints. Our culture also conveys messages via different media—television, radio, the Internet.

We give the people who communicate via these media far too much power in our lives. We are influenced and guided by what news reporters or shock jocks think far more than we care to admit.

How can we take back the control of our own minds? Perhaps by fasting for a time from the media. What if you spent an entire twenty-four hours emancipated from having to know what is going on everywhere, from the Middle East to the bathroom of an acquaintance who posts potty training updates on Facebook? Do you really need all that information?

In a recent *Sunset* magazine article, novelist Anne Lamott argues for taking the half hour or more we spend each day watching the news and investing it in something more fulfilling, like writing or enjoying your family. "This is what I say: First of all, no one needs to watch the news every night, unless one is married to the anchor. Otherwise, you are mostly going to learn more than you need to know about where the local fires are, and how rainy it has been: so rainy!"[18]

Simplicity is not beyond your reach. It may be as close as the off button on the remote control.

TODAY'S CHALLENGE

On a day when you don't have to go to work, take a twenty-four-hour fast from media and electronics. (This takes away the excuse of "needing" to be on the Internet or e-mail for work.) This is your chance to unplug—to experience real things instead of virtual ones, to connect with people face-to-face instead of through Facebook and Twitter.

You may want to begin your fast at sunset. Turn off the TV and enjoy your evening meal with friends or family. Actually talk to them. Go to sleep without the aid of television or movies. Refrain from watching television, reading the newspaper, listening to the radio, or even logging on to your computer for twenty-four hours. If you start in the evening, you'll be nearly halfway through your twenty-four hours by the time you wake up!

Plan some simple activities to substitute for electronic stimulation. Take a walk. Write a letter to a friend you haven't talked to in a while, and send it via "snail mail." Have a conversation with a friend—in person. Read a book. Play a board game with real people instead of a video game with virtual opponents. Sit outside and listen to the birds. This is a fast that may feel like deprivation but actually is freedom. I do this on a regular basis, and I can tell you that I've found much more peace in my life—and I haven't missed hearing about the latest crisis in the Middle East.

_____ *Check here when you have completed today's God Challenge.*

Notes

Day Eight

An Attitude of Gratitude

Joy is the serious business of heaven.[19]

—C. S. Lewis

If you are a parent, you know that one of the greatest joys of parenting is when your children say, "thank you." Whether they are thanking you for a gift, for time spent with them, or the car keys, you feel affirmed and connected. Any parent treasures a Father's Day or Mother's Day card that expresses appreciation and gratitude.

If you are not a parent, you still understand the value of saying thank you. When your boss says, "Good job!" or your friends say, "I appreciate your help," it means a lot. In fact, you could argue that gratitude is one of the ways in which we strengthen relationships. You also know that saying thank you transforms the "thanker." When we express gratitude, our world somehow brightens. Gratitude, when it is sincere, actually makes us more joyful. Gratitude, whether we are expressing it or having it expressed to us, allows us to experience love.

But sometimes we need a little help "getting our grateful on." We have to *decide* to be thankful, even if we're feeling grumpy. We have to count our blessings rather than overlooking or ignoring them. The blessings do exist, even though they seem subtle or hidden in times of struggle. Sometimes we have to change our perspective and look for the good. We need to see the glass half full instead of half empty.

In his classic book *Too Busy Not to Pray,* pastor and author Bill Hybels outlines a well-loved "pattern for prayer." He suggests, as others have, to pray following this acronym: ACTS. The letters stand for *Adoration, Confession, Thanksgiving,* and *Supplication.* Most of us, even if we use this pattern, tend to skip quickly through the first three to get to the heart of the matter— what we need God to do for us. We're thankful for his help, but we often don't take time to tell him that. "Some of us have not made a simple distinction," Hybels writes. "There is a difference between feeling grateful and expressing thanks." [20]

When we express thanks, we actually feel more joyful. And who wouldn't want that? Life can be stressful and overwhelming. We long for joy. What we sometimes don't realize is that joy can be found in the deliberate expression of gratitude. By naming our blessings, we change our thinking, and that changes our experience. We become happier people. By thanking God for those blessings, we experience his presence more fully.

John Ortberg writes: "Joy is God's basic character. Joy is his eternal destiny. God is the happiest being in the universe. . . . As products of God's creation, creatures made in his image, we are to reflect God's fierce joy in life." [21]

How can we reflect that fierce joy? By saying thank you. By recognizing that the blessings in our lives are not random luck, but the goodness of God expressed in tangible form.

Many of us wish our lives were more joyful. But do we realize that joylessness is actually a sin?

Ortberg continues: "The Bible puts joy in the non-optional category: Joy is a command. Joylessness is a serious sin, one that religious people are particularly prone to indulge in."

How often are you joyless? You may quickly protest: "If you knew my struggles, the difficulties I face, the stress I'm under, you'd understand why I'm not always joyful!" But the way to joy is not a problem-free life. The way to joy is through gratitude—not only felt gratitude, but gratitude that is expressed. *Joy is found when we look for things to be thankful for and express that thanks to God.*

🌿 TODAY'S CHALLENGE

Thankfulness should be a daily practice. But today you're going to engage in a bit of extended gratitude. Take out a piece of notebook paper or a journal. Start thinking about the things you are grateful for. Start with the easy stuff—family, friends, a job if you have one, good health if you have it, the fact that you are still here if you don't. What are some ways in which God has blessed you?

Hybels writes: "I thank God every day for four kinds of blessings: answered prayers, spiritual blessings, relational blessings and material blessings." [22]

Using these categories to get you started, begin writing. What prayers has God answered? What spiritual growth have you experienced? What spiritual blessings have you seen in the people you love that you want to thank God for? While at times we all face relational challenges, what things are going well relationally? And how has God provided for your material needs? If you have a roof over your head and a car to drive, you are wealthier than 98 percent of the world's population. Did you eat today? You're ahead of many people around the globe. Your job may be stressful, but if you have one, thank God for it.

Keep going. What else are you thankful for? Continue this gratitude exercise until you have filled up at least two pages of a journal or both sides of the notebook paper.

____ *Check here when you have completed today's God Challenge.*

Notes

Day Nine

Spiritual Mentors

Spiritual friends help us most when they make clear that their job is to point the way, not lead the way. And the Way to which they should point is Jesus.[23]

—David Benner

If you asked successful business leaders what contributed to their success, many would point to a mentor who helped them somewhere along the way. Their success is due, in part, to someone who encouraged them, made key introductions, steered them back when they started to get off track, or helped them think through strategies to build their business or career.

Likewise, many athletes at the top of their game would not be where they are without a coach who encouraged them, challenged them to train hard and make the most of their talent, and required them to develop mental and physical toughness.

Similarly, none of us goes on our spiritual journey alone. Even if you picked up the Bible one day on a whim, read it, believed it, and joined God's family on your own (a rare set of circumstances), others still guided you toward doing that. You may not have noticed them at the time, but they had influence—perhaps more than you know.

Think back to your childhood. Even if you grew up with atheists for parents, there were probably some people—maybe a neighbor, a coach, a teacher, even a peer—who encouraged you and had an impact on your life. God was working through that person, even though you may not have known it at the time. Now you can see clearly that he brought him or her into your life for a reason to point out the way for you as you began your journey.

Further along on your journey toward God, perhaps there was a colleague at work, a friend, a small-group leader, or even your spouse who prayed for you and introduced you to Jesus, giving you some simple guidance on how to invite him into your life.

We often talk about seeking God, but the Bible makes it very clear that God is always seeking us and wanting to have a close relationship with us. The Old Testament repeatedly tells us that God longs for us to seek and find him. In Jeremiah 29:12–14, God expresses his deep desire to connect with his people: " 'Then you will call upon me and come and pray to me, and I will listen to you. You will seek me and find me when you seek me with all your heart. I will be found by you,' declares the Lord" (see also Jeremiah 31:33; Ezekiel 14:11).

How does God draw us to himself? Most often, he does it through other people. Whether they pray for us, talk to us, or just love us, God connects with us through them.

This is important for two reasons: *First,* when we feel alone and ask, "Where is God?" we must remember that he is with us, in the hearts of the people around us who care for us. God is everywhere, as Spirit. The Bible says even the beauty of nature declares God's existence. (See Psalm 19:1.) But that same Spirit also lives in people and inspires them to love and serve. Where is God? He's in the people who love him, who are right in front of you.

And *second,* it reminds us that we must rise to the challenge of receiving God's love and then allowing it to flow through us toward others. If we can experience God's presence through another person, if that person can even lead us to faith in Christ, then we can do the same for others. Your purpose in life, in part, is to be a conduit of God's love and wisdom so that you can tell others about him and share with them his power and strength.

🌲 Today's Challenge

Think back to your first steps toward faith. Who were your spiritual mentors? Did someone answer your questions of doubt, read the Bible with you, point out the way to Jesus to you? Who discipled you as you took your first steps as a new believer?

Today, your challenge is to sit down and write a letter to the person or people who led you to Christ. Whether it was a pastor, friend, or parent, let them know that you are grateful for the way they mentored you, for the guidance they provided.

Perhaps it was one person, or maybe it was several people who pointed out the next step in the spiritual journey for you. Write to each person who played a significant role in your journey toward God, telling them how much you appreciate what they did in your life.

It may be that the person who led you to Christ is no longer living. That's okay. Write a letter anyway, perhaps in a journal. Put down in black-and-white how much you appreciate them and what you would tell them if you could.

____ *Check here when you have completed today's God Challenge.*

Notes

DAY TEN

Friends

Friendship is the greatest of worldly goods. Certainly to me it is the chief happiness of life.[24]

—C. S. LEWIS

The U.S. Census Bureau says that the average American will move 11.7 times in their lifetime. Other sources say the average family moves every five to seven years. According to the Bureau of Labor Statistics, the average American worker changes jobs every four years.

Those statistics translate into scenes like this: a moving truck in your neighbor's driveway, tearful good-byes between the kids who've become best friends, a tug at your heart as the person you finally felt connected with moves away. Or, your employer says that to keep your job you have to relocate. Or, you find the perfect job in another city and you must say good-bye to co-workers and neighbors. You move to a new town, find a new church, make new friends. Life starts over in a new place.

I know what that's like. At the time of this writing, I've been married twenty-seven years, and we've moved about seventeen times. Ugh. Our culture is transitory. People you were close to five or ten years ago may not even be on your Christmas card list anymore. As a result, it is very easy to keep your relationships at a surface level. Our transience and our loneliness may be related.

While it is virtually impossible to keep in touch with every friend you've ever had, long-term friendships have great value. People who've known you for a long time know the real you—or at least more than people you've just met. It's harder to hide your faults from them, and while this may be disconcerting, it's also comforting—*they know all about you but are your friends anyway.*

When Jesus came to earth, he did not remain isolated, appearing randomly to preach and heal. Rather, he gathered a small group of people around him and built deep friendships. Although he was their leader and they were his followers (disciples), Jesus told them: "I no longer call you servants, because a servant does not know his master's business. Instead, I have called you friends, for everything that I learned from my Father I have made known to you" (John 15:15).

While some turnover in our friendships is inevitable, Jesus modeled friendship that went much deeper than mere acquaintance. If we are following him and trying to live as he would if he were in our place, then we must be willing to forge deeper friendships. We must seek out and maintain what some people call "soul friendships."

In his book *Sacred Companions,* Dr. David Benner writes about spiritual friendships—those that go beyond the surface, that are focused on helping one another grow closer to God. He writes:

By daring to be honest with us, friends offer us invaluable opportunities for growth. They can help us penetrate our self-deceptions and cherished illusions. Just as the retina of the human eye contains a blind spot, so too, the human soul contains a blind spot. Soul friends help us see things we cannot see on our own. . . . Soul friends want each other to settle for nothing short of becoming the whole and holy person they are called to be.[25]

Some of us read words like that and are filled with a longing—we want friendships like that but perhaps have not experienced them. We feel uncertain about how to build such relationships. Maybe we have moved more than the average person and never had a chance to practice building long-term relationships. Or we're scared to try, for any number of reasons.

The old wisdom "to find a friend, you must be a friend" is still true. If you are looking for friends as a method of social climbing, you'll be disappointed. Rather than focusing on yourself, look for someone who needs a friend—there are plenty of lonely people all around you. I'll bet your church has some lonely attendees, and I know the local retirement home has some folks who would love a visit.

C. S. Lewis wrote that while romantic love is focused on each other, friendship is focused on a common activity, idea, or goal. A friend is someone who is more than just an acquaintance or companion. He wrote:

Friendship arises out of mere companionship when two or more of the companions discover that they have in common some insight or interest or even taste, which the others do not share and which, till that moment, each believed to be his own unique treasure (or burden). The typical expression of opening a friendship would be something like, "What? You, too? I thought I was the only one."[26]

🌳 Today's Challenge

Do you have someone who was once a "soul friend"? Someone who was close to you at one time? Spend some time praying for that person today.

Then get in touch with her. Call her, send an e-mail, or even an old-fashioned "snail mail" letter. Tell your friend that you're praying for her. Ask how she is doing and how you can continue to pray for her. Let her know how much you value the impact she has had on your life.

If you wish you had a deeper friendship in your life, spend some time praying about that. Do you have a friend currently in your life that has the potential to go deeper? Someone who might be looking to have more honesty and accountability in a relationship? Pray for an opportunity to talk with that person about how to take your friendship to another level—perhaps by agreeing to pray for each other.

_____ *Check here when you have completed today's God Challenge.*

Notes

Sing a New Song

*Hymn singing, far from being an ornament or decoration
to Christian worship and the life of faith, is intrinsic to
the worship and faith experience.*[27]

—DON E. SALIERS

Imagine watching a movie with no soundtrack. Although sometimes we're not consciously aware of the background music in a film, it often stirs our emotions in a way that action and dialogue alone cannot. Try, for example, to imagine Rocky running up the steps of the museum raising his arms, without the victorious "da-dat-DAAAHH, da-dat-DAAAHHH" accompanying his run. Try to imagine the girl swimming in the ocean, the great white shark getting ready to attack, without the "DUH-nuh-nuh-nuh, DUH-nuh-nuh-nuh . . ." of the *Jaws* theme song playing in the background.

Movies use music to create an emotional response—the music often crescendos in tandem with the action or emotion on screen. It forces us to engage; it draws us in. Music touches us in a way that spoken words cannot.

Hearing a song that you associate with a certain person or time in your life can make you feel happy or sad, nostalgic or nervous. God made us this way, to have an emotional response to music. I believe it's no accident that the longest book of the Bible, Psalms, is essentially a hymnal—a book of songs to be sung in times of joy or sorrow. And that same book instructs us to worship God by singing: "Sing to the Lord a new song; sing to the Lord, all the earth. Sing to the Lord, praise his name; proclaim his salvation day after day" (Psalm 96:1–2).

Even on the night of the Last Supper, Jesus and his disciples concluded their meal by singing a hymn. It had to have been a somber moment, but certainly one they did not soon forget.

The church has always used music to help people connect with God and to communicate truth about God. Words set to music are easier to remember, and so the great hymns have been a tool for communicating truth in a way that people will not only enjoy but also remember. Most likely, even if you don't think you're good at memorizing, you have hundreds of song lyrics stored in your brain. The question is, are any of those lyrics to Christian songs or hymns?

We all have days when we don't feel like praising God. We'd rather complain about how hard our life has become and how many of our needs he seems to be ignoring. The Bible tells us to rejoice always (see Philippians 4:4), but that's sometimes hard to do. *Often, the best way to change your mood from complaining to rejoicing is by singing.*

When we engage in the practice of singing, it can actually change our perspective. It's hard to sing about joy and not feel a little more joyful as a result.

Don E. Saliers writes, "The act of singing together is deeply and indelibly human. When we sing, words are given greater range and power than when we speak."[28]

Many worship songs are based on Bible verses, so learning a song can be a way to memorize Scripture. When we begin to make hymns or Christian choruses the soundtrack of our lives, we'll find that God will bring a song to mind that fits our situation. In times of struggle, words of reassurance will echo through our minds. When we feel joyful, words of praise will flow.

🌳 TODAY'S CHALLENGE

Is worship music a part of your life? Do you only hear it at church once a week? Or do you listen to Christian radio or CDs? Whether you like classical, rap, or something in between, Christian artists have created music in your favorite genre. Go online, or visit a Christian bookstore, and do a little exploring of various kinds of Christian music.

If you grew up in a church that sang hymns, you probably know more of them than you realize. Hymns like "Amazing Grace," "A Mighty Fortress Is Our God," "Great Is Thy Faithfulness," or "Joyful, Joyful We Adore Thee" are a few titles you may know. Again, you can find Web sites that have hymn lyrics if you need a little help.

Today's challenge is to spend some time worshiping God by singing. On your way to work, if you drive by yourself, sing hymns and spiritual songs. If you don't know many, tune in to a Christian music station or bring a CD to sing along with.

If you're in a carpool, you may want to bring a Christian music CD and ask if your fellow carpoolers would mind listening to it. Singing is optional in a carpool (and I wouldn't recommend it unless you have a really good voice and don't mind sharing it).

If you commute on a train, load your MP3 player with worship songs and listen to it during your ride to work. (Again, singing out loud on the train may not be something you want to do . . . unless you want some strange looks.) Even if you listen in silence, pray the words you hear in your heart.

_____ *Check here when you have completed today's God Challenge.*

Notes

Some Time With Jesus

> *The Bible is not pieces of information about God and Jesus and whatever else we take and apply to situations as we would a cookbook or an instruction manual. . . . We have to embrace the Bible as the wild, uncensored, passionate account it is of people experiencing the living God.*[29]
>
> —ROB BELL

Have you ever watched a really great movie or read an engrossing novel and gotten completely lost in the story? As you watched or read, it was as if you were actually getting to know the characters, spending time with them as their adventures unfolded. Even after you turned the last page or got to the end of the movie, you still thought about the characters and wished you could learn more about them.

That's the power of story—when a story is well-told, we don't feel as if we know *about* the characters. We feel like we actually *know* them.

That's why so much of the Bible is written in story form. While the Bible also has some lists of rules, explanations of theology, poetry, and songs, most of it is narrative. And with very little effort, we can engage with it in such a way that we feel as if we are actually getting to know the people whose lives are described within its pages.

The problem is we often read short snippets of the Bible—sometimes from our "verse-a-day" calendar or a devotional. While there are times when it is appropriate, even spiritually transforming to reflect on a short portion of Scripture and really ponder it deeply, there are also times when reading larger blocks of the story can be helpful. *When we read longer sections, we see the big picture and the themes that run consistently through the whole book.*

I often hear Christians say they wish they'd lived when Jesus walked the earth. They wonder aloud what it would have been like to sit on a Judean hillside and listen to the Sermon on the Mount as Jesus actually gave it. To eat a bit of bread and fish that had miraculously been multiplied. To sit in a boat and watch Jesus walk on water or calm a storm with a word. They seem to imply that if they had actually seen Jesus in the flesh, they might wrestle with doubt a little less; they might be more dedicated to their faith.

But the thing is—we *can* spend time with Jesus, because we have the Gospels. We have his story, written from four different perspectives, recorded for us by eyewitnesses and friends, so that we can get to know him better. If we want to spend time with Jesus, we need only open the book that contains his story, and begin to read it.

For centuries, Christians have engaged with the Gospels through a spiritual practice known as Gospel Meditation or the Ignatian Method (so called because St. Ignatius of Loyola recommended this practice to his followers). Don't let either name throw you—this is simply a spiritual discipline of reading carefully and *thinking about what you're reading* enough to imagine yourself in the story.

The Bible instructs us to meditate on God's Word, which means thinking about and pondering Bible truth. (See Psalm 1.) When you read the Bible, do you skim it? Or do you dissect it, analyzing each word and phrase? Or do you try to engage in the story? What would happen if you imagined yourself in the story, perhaps in the place of one of the disciples? What sights, sounds, and feelings would you experience as you watched Jesus heal people, or heard him teach?

The truth is, rather than wishing we had been born in first-century Palestine, we can spend time with Jesus by reading the Gospels in this way. We have the added benefit of the gift of the Holy Spirit, who helps us to understand the Bible and gives us insights we would not have on our own.

TODAY'S CHALLENGE

Many of us have preconceived notions of what Jesus was like as a man. We may think of him as rather mild. Reading through a gospel can remind us how confrontational, strong, and even obscure he sometimes could be.

Today, your challenge is to sit down and read one of the Gospels in its entirety. So you must decide two things: which one of the four you will read, and in which version.

Which of the Gospels have you read or studied the least? Which of the four—Matthew, Mark, Luke, or John—is less familiar to you than the others? Perhaps you will want to select that gospel for your reading today. (Mark is the easiest to get through, Luke the most fun to read, John is gentlest and the one that feels different from the other three.)

Find a version of the Bible that is perhaps less familiar to you. You may want to try the old-fashioned English of the King James Version (if, like me, you enjoy reading Shakespeare in your spare time, you'll probably like it). Or you may want to pick up a more modern version that puts the Bible into plain English, such as *The Message* paraphrase or the *New Living Translation*. Another more modern and easy-to-read version is the J. B. Phillips translation. (If you don't own a hard copy of one of these versions, you can find them online.)

As you read, imagine yourself in the action—listen to what Jesus says, notice how he treats people. And notice your response to the story—the particular places you resonate with it, or the places you shake your head or resist it. Both resonance and resistance point us toward something God may be trying to tell us.

Ponder Jesus' sometimes strange actions and words. Marvel at his wisdom and compassion. Imagine that Jesus is talking to you, listening to you, healing you. When you have finished reading, spend a few minutes in prayer, talking to Jesus, whom you now know better than you did before.

_____ *Check here when you have completed today's God Challenge.*

Notes

_____

_____

_____

_____

DAY THIRTEEN

Anonymous Giving

Good will come to him who is generous and lends freely,
who conducts his affairs with justice.

—PSALM 112:5

In August 2010, the following item appeared in the *New York Times*:

> More than three dozen billionaires, including well-known philanthropists like David Rockefeller and Mayor Michael R. Bloomberg of New York and less familiar big donors like Lorry I. Lokey, founder of Business Wire, have promised at least half of their fortunes to charity, joining a program that Bill and Melinda Gates and Warren Buffett started in June to encourage other wealthy people to give.

The article speculated about the effect such giving would have on charitable organizations. It also quoted Larry Ellison, the founder of computer giant Oracle, one of the billionaires signing Buffett's pledge. Ellison disclosed for the first time that he had previously given away millions of dollars and put 95 percent of his wealth in a charitable trust, but had done so without fanfare "because I have long believed that charitable giving is a personal and private matter." However, at Buffett's request, Ellison was going public to try to inspire others. "I hope he's right," Ellison told the *Times*.[30]

So my question is, was Buffett right? Are you inspired by this story? Or do you think it's easy for billionaires to give away half their wealth because the other half is still more than most people would ever dream of having? While I applaud the steps Warren Buffett and Bill and Melinda Gates have taken to try to use their wealth for good in the world, I am more inspired by a story in the Bible, which tells of a different sort of giving.

The billionaires of Jesus' day were making a big show of dropping sacks of money into the collection box at the temple, hoping to impress. Maybe they told themselves that they were "setting an example" for others, encouraging them to be generous.

A poor woman snuck up to the box and dropped in two small coins. As she crept away, Jesus said to the people around him (including those wealthy donors), "This poor widow has put in more than all the others. All these people gave their gifts out of their wealth; but she out of her poverty put in all she had to live on" (Luke 21:3–4).

Jesus looked not at the outward actions, but at the heart. *Giving not only transforms the recipient, it transforms the giver.* When we give out of our excess, it may help someone else a bit but it doesn't help us very much at all.

I wonder what Jesus would say to those billionaires who got written up in the *Times*. Another time Jesus said, "So when you give to the needy, do not announce it with trumpets, as the hypocrites do in the synagogues and on the streets, to be honored by men" (Matthew 6:2).

This verse contains two important theological concepts. First, Jesus does not say "*if* you give" but rather "*when* you give." Jesus assumes that we will be generous, that we will not hoard all that we have, but share it with others. Second, he advocates giving "in secret" (see Matthew 6:1–4). Giving is not to be announced, but done without fanfare.

Giving anonymously is a spiritually transforming experience. Because the recipient cannot thank you, they more readily attribute the gift to its ultimate source, God. So when you give anonymously, you point people to God, without their realizing that it's you who's doing the pointing. Often, such gifts will bolster someone's faith or pay a bill they had no other way to pay. It's thrilling to be a part of meeting someone's needs in that way without letting anyone know.

Other times, you might give anonymously and never find out how your gift impacted the recipient. That's okay. Giving in this way is an act of obedience. It's enough to know that you have obeyed God's commands to be generous.

🌳 Today's Challenge

Today, follow the example of the poor widow, and the commands of Scripture, and give generously and anonymously. Give even if you are uncertain about your own finances.

The way we handle our money is a true test of the authenticity of our faith. If we say we follow Jesus, would our checkbook be evidence of that claim?

Begin by praying, asking God earnestly to show you where to give your gift. Do you know of someone who is in financial need right now? Or perhaps you know of a charity that does good work for the poor.

Then pray about an amount. As a minimum, give at least $50. If you could afford this book, you can give $50 to someone— even though it may be a bit of a stretch. Ask God if he wants you to give more than that, and if you feel so led, obey fearlessly.

To keep your gift anonymous, give cash, or get a cashier's check that doesn't have to have your name on it. Give your gift without anyone knowing who gave it. Don't keep any record of it for your tax return. Don't tell anyone else about this gift. See what God will do with your secret gift. See the joy that comes from giving anonymously.

_____ *Check here when you have completed today's God Challenge.*

Notes

In Other Words . . .

The book of Psalms offers a practicum in how to pray. . . .
Fear, praise, anxiety, anger, love, sorrow, despair, gratitude,
grief, doubt, suffering, joy, vengeance, repentance—every
human emotion and experience surges to the surface in the
prayer-poems of Psalms.[31]

—PHILIP YANCEY

Do you ever wrestle with what to say to God when you pray? Do you wonder if he's listening, or if he's even there? Do you stumble over the words or get distracted and forget what you were saying?

I often feel inarticulate when I'm on my knees. I skirt the issues. I hem and haw. I blurt things out without thinking. I lose track of what I'm saying. I think, "If I'm this bored, how must God feel listening to me babble on?" Thank God, literally, for grace, because I need it when I pray.

As we have pointed out earlier, the longest book of the Bible is Psalms, a collection of songs and prayers and poems. They offer us examples of prayers for almost any situation, prayers for times of joy as well as sorrow, repentance as well as anger.

The psalms are meant to be read, but also to be *used*. We can pray them as they are, or we can use them as a model for how to pray.

Prayer is, of course, an important spiritual discipline. But as you will see continuing in the God Challenge, *prayer can take many forms*. And while it is, in some ways, a very natural thing to do, we can always learn more. The psalms are an ideal place to go to school on prayer.

Some psalms were written to be prayed in groups as a liturgy. Others are labeled "a song of ascents," and they are most often psalms of praise and thanksgiving. Still others are psalms of lament, expressing grief or even anger at God. Each is appropriate at certain times in our lives.

The psalms of lament, one commentary notes, were written as "models of prayer composed for the generic needs of God's people. In this respect, a lament psalm is not a mirror reflecting the composer's experience; rather, it provides worshipers a framework to interpret their own experiences and to guide their expressions of prayer."[32]

Not all psalms express sadness, of course. Many offer thanksgiving and praise, affirming the goodness of God. Nor should we always turn to the lament psalms when we feel unhappy or disappointed. Sometimes simple words like, "I will bless the Lord at all times: his praise shall continually be in my mouth" (Psalm 34:1 KJV) or "Give thanks to the Lord, for he is good; his love endures forever" (Psalm 118:1) will lift our spirits and affirm the truth.

Sometimes, the psalms become even more meaningful when we make them our own. Students are said to have mastered a subject when they don't simply parrot information, but can put the ideas they are learning into their own words. Similarly, we will strengthen our grip on God's truth when we can paraphrase it, making it personal and specific.

A great model for how to do this is found in *The Message* paraphrase of the Bible. For example, in the NIV, Psalm 42 begins:

> As the deer pants for streams of water,
>   so my soul pants for you, O God.
> My soul thirsts for God, for the living God.
>   When can I go and meet with God?

The same verses in *The Message* read:

> A white-tailed deer drinks from the creek;
> I want to drink God,
>   deep draughts of God.
> I'm thirsty for God-alive.
> I wonder, "Will I ever make it—
>   arrive and drink in God's presence?"

🌱 Today's Challenge

How are you feeling today? What's going on with you and God? Do you feel close to him? Long to praise him? Or are you wondering why he seems absent or distant? Be honest as you assess what's going on spiritually.

Today, your goal is not to try to change how you feel toward God, but to write a prayer that expresses what it is. You are going to write a prayer using a psalm as a model. In other words, you will paraphrase a psalm: put it into your own words, as if you were writing it to God. Then you will make these words your prayer.

Begin by selecting a psalm. To find one, take some time to page through the Psalms. If you have a favorite, or one that you know expresses your current spiritual situation, you may want to choose that one.

What is the psalm saying? How can you put it into different words, your own words? First put down some ideas, then go back and revise it if you want. When you are finished, read your psalm aloud as a prayer to God.

_____ *Check here when you have completed today's God Challenge.*

Notes

Gathered in His Name

Has it ever occurred to you that one hundred pianos all tuned to the same fork are automatically tuned to each other? They are of one accord by being tuned, not to each other, but to another standard to which each one must individually bow.[33]

—A. W. TOZER

There is a certain irony in the fact that people who live in the country with the most advanced communications system in the world often find themselves much more lonely and isolated than those in less "advanced" cultures. Many of our ways of staying in touch are electronic, and as a result we are starving for authentic community.

The church is meant to be a community of believers, but it doesn't always function in this way. In part, this may be because the American version of Christianity differs most profoundly from biblical Christianity in this way: it assumes that community is something we engage in for an hour on Sunday. The rest of the week, we are basically on our own: having a quiet time alone; going for a run alone with worship music on our MP3 player; spending time alone studying the Scriptures; and praying alone for our individual concerns.

The Bible, however, tells the story of the people of God: the *people* (plural). It tells the story of the birth and growth of the church, which is a community. Acts 1:14 describes the church before Pentecost in this way: "They all joined together constantly in prayer, along with the women and Mary the mother of Jesus, and with his brothers." Faith was not a lonely walk, and prayer was something you joined others in as much as you engaged in it alone.

Of course, sometimes solitude is necessary—Jesus modeled that. But he also modeled community. Certainly he prayed with his disciples. The Gospels tell the story of a time Jesus' disciples came to him when he was praying, and asked that he teach them how to pray.

The way Jesus answered their question implies that he expected that some of their prayers would be corporate. His model prayer uses all plural pronouns: "*our* father," "*our* bread," "forgive *us*," and so on. He does not tell them to pray "*my* father" or "give me *my* daily bread." *Christ seems to assume that his followers would gather and pray corporately and also that they would pray unselfishly. That they would pray with and for one another, that us and our would be the logical pronouns to use.*

Matthew 18 sets up some ground rules for community and encourages believers to work things out in community. It offers guidelines for conflict resolution, for interpreting Scripture, and for forgiving each other when we've failed one another. It also promises God's presence when Christians pray together. Jesus says, "Again, truly I tell you, if two of you agree on earth about anything you ask, it will be done for you by my Father in heaven. For where two or three are gathered in my name, I am there among them" (Matthew 18:19–20 NRSV).

Likewise, the entire book of 1 John focuses on how God's love is made manifest in our love for one another. In fact, it says that God's love is made complete in our love for our neighbors. And one of the ways we can show that love is to pray with others.

Throughout the New Testament, we find the words *one another* in phrases like "encourage one another," or "love one another," and certainly "pray for one another." Christianity is a "one another" faith—a journey we simply cannot take alone.

🌱 Today's Challenge

Many of us squirm at the idea of praying out loud. We have mistakenly assumed that prayer of this sort is a performance by which we will be judged. We worry what others will think. But we are missing the point. It's more like two of Jesus' disciples coming to him to talk about a problem they're having or to thank him for some amazing thing he has done in their life. It is a conversation, not a contest.

Today, your challenge is to pray with others. Is there a prayer chain set up for your church or small group? Is there a system in place for sharing with others the petitions of these brothers and sisters? Or perhaps there is a prayer group meeting which you have avoided in the past. It's time to revisit this discipline. Many people meet for prayer, both in the church and outside of it— moms at schools, co-workers at businesses, even schoolchildren during their lunch hour! Praying with our brothers and sisters in Christ reminds us of the tie that binds us together as Christ's bride, the church, a living, breathing body of which you are a part.

God hears our prayers, and he hears them when we pray on our own as well as when we meet with a friend. Yet there is incredible power in meeting together in greater numbers. And with the advent of e-mail, Facebook, and all the other social media options available, we are more connected than ever before. Let's take the opportunity to use these ties to bind our hearts together in prayer.

____ *Check here when you have completed today's God Challenge.*

Notes

Day Sixteen

Older and Wiser

The glory of young men is their strength,
gray hair the splendor of the old.

—Proverbs 20:29

It's been said that being loved and being listened to feel so similar that most people cannot tell the difference between the two. So if the mark of a Christian is love, then one way we can become more loving is to become better listeners.

As a seminary student, I spent one Sunday afternoon each month at the local nursing home, preaching and leading a little church service, if you could call it that. I wanted a forgiving audience as I practiced preaching, and figured correctly that the nursing home residents would not object to any visitor, even me. I thought I was learning to preach, but I was actually learning to listen.

I was pleasantly surprised at how much I came to enjoy those Sunday afternoons. We'd gather in a room that had an old, out-of-tune upright piano, dutifully played by a scrawny, scowling woman who'd pound on that keyboard and never smile. I'm sure she had a story, but she was not sharing it with me or any of the residents.

We'd sing the residents' favorite old hymns, the ones they'd grown up singing: "The Old Rugged Cross," "A Mighty Fortress Is Our God," "He Walks With Me," and "Great Is Thy Faithfulness."

Though their bodies were old and broken, many had sweet spirits. One older gentleman was confined to a wheelchair. Had he been able to stand, he would have been very tall; now he couldn't even hold his head up straight. But what he lacked in physical strength he made up for in enthusiasm. He had been a pastor in his younger days, and he knew *all* the words to *all* the songs— including *all* the verses.

In fact, most of them had committed every verse of those old songs to memory. Of course, there was one woman who knew all the words, and loved to play the piano and sing, but she kept forgetting which hymns we'd already sung that day. As a result, it wasn't unusual to sing "To God Be the Glory" about six times in one afternoon. None of the other residents raised any objection. Another old woman always carried a baby doll with her and treated it like it was a real baby.

Still, these people ministered to me as I tried to minister to them. Their bodies were weak, but their spirits were commensurately strong. They knew God, and his love, in a profound way. They seemed to live out Psalm 46:10: "Cease striving and know that I am God" (NASB). A couple of the older women were very faithful prayer warriors who remained positive even though they were frail and didn't get many visitors. I remember one dear woman telling me she didn't mind the fact that she had all those hours alone, because she loved all the time that gave her to pray.

Visiting with those folks was an important spiritual practice for me, especially as a young seminary student who thought I had all the answers or at least that I would obtain them along with my master's degree. I began to see that most of the deepest truths of

God cannot be learned from books but only by walking with him for a lifetime. *And I saw that the ministry of my sermons was not nearly as important as the ministry of my attention—simple words of encouragement meant much more than deep words of the scholar.* People at the nursing home listened to my preaching probably with greater attentiveness than it deserved, but what really communicated God's love to them was when they would talk to me afterward, and I would listen.

Other cultures around the world (and throughout history), including the culture in which the Bible was written, have honored the elderly. Our culture generally does not. In addition to always seeking to stay young, we're also very focused on productivity, which often seems to slow down as a person gets older—they're not as "useful" or productive, and therefore have less value in our eyes. Our dual obsession with youthfulness and productivity means that people who are old and no longer contributing financially lose our respect. This is a dangerous way to think. First, it causes us to miss out on the wisdom and strength gained through experience that older people can offer. But second, it reinforces our illusion that God loves us because of what we can do for him. When we see people who can't do all that much (in our eyes), we are confronted with the truth that God's love truly is unconditional, and our accomplishments mean very little to him. What he wants is our heart.

🌳 Today's Challenge

A generation ago, aging parents often lived with their adult children when they could no longer live independently. Today, most are in retirement centers or nursing homes. As a result, many of us are not used to interacting with elderly people. But the Bible tells us to treat older people with respect. (See 1 Timothy 5:1.)

One way to do that is to visit a nursing home, which is an excellent place to practice loving by listening. Elderly folks forget details, repeat things, and at times tell stories that don't relate to our lives. But they are lonely, and we need to make time to love them by listening to their stories, however rambling they may be.

Today, your challenge is to go and visit a nursing home. Ask the staff to direct you to someone who does not typically get visitors, and visit that person. Ask if he or she would like you to read Scripture (the Psalms are often a favorite) or pray with them. Go with the intention to listen. Your quiet attention ministers far more deeply than you realize. Ask questions about their life, their opinions, and then *listen*. Let people talk, even if you feel like it's a waste of time. It allows them to feel valuable and a part of the community again. Learning to ask questions so that they'll talk is a valuable lesson.

_____ *Check here when you have completed today's God Challenge.*

Notes

Your Whole Self

> God is not interested in your "spiritual life." God is just interested in your life. He intends to redeem it.[34]
>
> —JOHN ORTBERG

It's easy to compartmentalize your life—to think of your spiritual life as one piece, your work life as another, your physical experience as yet another piece of the pie that you tend to as needed, then set aside. The problem with such an approach is that you can easily assume that ignoring one piece won't have any impact on the rest.

Simple experience shows that such thinking is faulty. Your spiritual, physical, mental, and emotional lives cannot be separated. Each part impacts the other in significant ways. If you sit around watching TV and eating junk food all day, you're going to feel sluggish; and rather quickly, your mental health is going to deteriorate—you move from bored to unmotivated, even depressed. As your brain and body go soft, your spiritual life will degenerate. An "Oh, well" mentality will pervade not only your physical efforts but your spiritual strength as well. On the other hand, when you tend to your physical health, it has a positive impact on your mental health, your work life, and your relationships—including your relationship with God. He wants to redeem your whole self, not merely one little religious piece of you. *He is interested in your life—all of it. Not pieces of it.*

The Christian faith is integrative. Just as your relationship with God should influence all of your actions and decisions, so your actions and decisions influence your relationship with God. Your health and fitness are no exception.

God created our bodies, and our bodies house our souls. If you're a believer, your body is home to not only your soul but God's Spirit. The apostle Paul wrote: "Do you not know that your body is a temple of the Holy Spirit, who is in you, whom you have received from God? You are not your own; you were bought at a price. Therefore honor God with your body" (1 Corinthians 6:19–20).

In this particular passage, Paul was talking about sexual purity. But the principles apply also to physical fitness, and what we put into our bodies as far as food, drink, and other substances. If our body is ruled by addictions, whether they are addictions to food, drink, drugs, or even visual images that we take into our body and brain through our eyes, we are refusing to honor God with our bodies.

At the opposite end of the spectrum are people who are so enthused about health and fitness that it can become an addiction, or at least an obsession. Focus solely on the physical, and it leads to narcissism. Again, an integrative approach is best. Maintaining your health is not done for its own sake, but so that you can be mentally and spiritually strong so that you can make good decisions in other areas of your life.

In another passage, Paul wrote: "For physical training is of some value, but godliness has value for all things, holding promise for both the present life and the life to come" (1 Timothy 4:8). Disciplines have value, whether it is the discipline of exercise or the discipline of prayer. I often find that my daily run not only helps me stay healthy physically, but the discipline of it makes me stronger mentally.

The Psalms say that we are "fearfully and wonderfully made" (139:14). The human body is an engineering marvel if you think about the mechanics of it, the coordination of many complex systems. Think of all the intricate muscles, nerves, and tendons that must work in tandem simply to hit a baseball or even to sit and read this book.

Consider that phrase—"wonderfully made." How often do you marvel or wonder at how God made your body? Physical activity also allows us to be playful—to enjoy and wonder at the world and all that God has made, including us.

The Bible says that one mark of the Holy Spirit in our lives is joy. But you can't get more joyful by just powering up. Joy is the kind of thing that can't be forced—it comes when we stop looking for it.

I'm a type A personality. I work, then work some more, then take a break so I can do other work. I have to run every morning to break out of sitting at my desk sending e-mails and talking on the phone. Sometimes I forget to have fun, and I have to be reminded that there is joy in going for a walk on the beach, or attending a baseball game, or swinging a golf club at the driving range (I am the world's worst golfer).

Are you an "all work and no play" type of person? Or does your recreation consist of watching other people play sports? Perhaps you need to engage in physical activity for no other reason than this: It would be fun, and you need to increase your joy level.

🌱 Today's Challenge

Today, your challenge is to get some exercise. No need for equipment or a gym membership—take some time and go for a walk. Alone or with a friend, or even with your dog. If you're up to it, go for a run. If you do have a club membership at a gym or a pool, go and work out. If you're exercising alone, load up your MP3 player with upbeat worship music to listen to as you exercise. If the weather's bad, dance around your living room, or walk up and down the stairs for a while.

If you have children, play with your kids. They'll enjoy it and you'll enjoy them. (I've long thought that a guy who wrestles with his kids once a week will one day win votes for "Father of the Year.") Being playful takes a certain amount of humility—you have to be willing to be silly, to let down your guard and not take yourself too seriously. Such humility can be spiritually forming in profound ways, if you let it.

Allow yourself to have fun. Really get into it, whether you are playing tag, throwing a ball, bouncing on a trampoline, jumping rope, or dancing around the living room with your three-year-old. You'll feel good and your kids will absolutely love it.

If you don't have kids, invite a friend to shoot some baskets or toss a football around. Exercise doesn't have to be serious and intense to be effective, especially when your primary goal is simply to have fun and increase your joy. You might not want to do this one—it's a physical exercise rather than a mental one. But right now, get up out of your chair and go DO something.

Then thank God that you have the ability to move, that you are strong and healthy enough to be able to exercise, even if all you can handle is a walk around the block. Remind yourself that your body is the temple of the Holy Spirit; then go enjoy the gift of health.

_____ *Check here when you have completed today's God Challenge.*

Notes

The Least of These

The great tragedy in the church is not that rich Christians do not care about the poor but that rich Christians do not know the poor.[35]

—Shane Claiborne

An acquaintance of mine took her daughter to the city one day to visit a museum. On the city sidewalks, the little girl encountered, for the first time in her young life, homeless people begging. She asked her mother about the people. Where did they live? Why were they asking for money? Why did it seem they hadn't had a bath in a long time?

The girl's questions made her mother very uncomfortable. She tried to explain that these people lived on the street, that they didn't have a home. She didn't know why and couldn't offer any explanation to her daughter. She didn't really want to think about it and hurried her daughter into the museum.

The little girl, however, couldn't stop thinking about the people on the streets and how cold they must get during the winter. So, because she was too young to think that she couldn't, she decided to do something about it.

She went back to her school out in the far edges of suburbia and asked her principal if she could organize a blanket drive for homeless people in the city. She went to her church and told her Sunday school teacher about the homeless people. She asked friends, family, and neighbors to donate blankets, and she collected quite a few.

Each December for the past several years (she started this when she was about eight years old), that girl has gone down to the city with her aunt (who offered to help with this project) with a pile of donated blankets and several thermoses full of hot chocolate. She stands on a corner and hands out blankets and a cup of hot chocolate, in Jesus' name.

It's a true story—I know that girl. I appreciate her spunk. Unlike her, we sometimes think that large societal problems like homelessness and poverty are much too complicated for us to do anything about. Or, in our ignorance, we assume that someone who has less privilege than we have is simply lazy. More often, we avoid thinking about it at all. We're too busy to learn anything about the circumstances and factors that keep people trapped in cycles of poverty, or the alarming rate at which mental institutions (due to loss of funding) are releasing patients who are not ready for independent living. We don't want to know how many homeless people are veterans who were damaged mentally and physically while fighting to protect our country.

We want to avoid the issue, so we work harder than we realize to protect our ignorance. While many homeless people will ask for money, this is not always the most helpful thing to give. It's hard to know which people are in genuine need, and which are professional panhandlers. Also, giving money can sometimes keep people in cycles of addiction and dependence.

Jesus once had a conversation with some religious people, and he told them that on judgment day, people will be separated into two groups: those who showed compassion to others, and those who didn't. Those who showed compassion will be welcomed into his kingdom, Jesus said, and they'll be welcomed with the following greeting: "For I was hungry and you gave me something to eat, I was thirsty and you gave me something to drink, I was a stranger and you invited me in" (Matthew 25:35). Those who did not do these things will be turned away into "eternal fire." And when they ask, "When did we see you hungry or thirsty?" Jesus says that he will reply: "Whatever you did not do for one of the least of these, you did not do for me" (Matthew 25:45).

It's a sobering passage, which reminds us that *faith* and *action* are to be seamlessly intertwined. Jesus said the most important things are to love God and love our neighbor. Many of us have arranged our lives so that we don't interact with people who are hungry, thirsty, homeless, or poor. And yet, just because such people are not often visible to us does not excuse us. *True compassion often means engaging enough to really know someone's story.* Those less fortunate are still our neighbors, and God is still calling us to love them in practical ways.

So how do we show compassion? Following Jesus' directives is a good start. Food, water, and clothing are basic needs. When we are generous with these things, it is as if we are being generous to Jesus himself.

🌱 TODAY'S CHALLENGE

Francis Chan, in his book *Crazy Love,* wrote, "God's definition of what matters is pretty straightforward. He measures our lives by how we love." [36]

How can we love people who are hungry, thirsty, or hurting? Grappling with this question is essential to our spiritual growth. Taking action toward loving the least of these is also essential.

If you know of a ministry that works with homeless people, you may want to have a conversation with someone who works in that ministry. Learn what you can about the problem of homelessness.

But today, your challenge is to find a place where the homeless typically congregate—perhaps a park, subway, or street corner.

Go to that place and offer to buy a meal for a homeless person. Or, like the little girl we mentioned earlier, you could give someone a blanket or a sleeping bag.

As an alternative, you may want to pack up some sandwiches, granola bars, and water bottles, and hand them out to people who are hungry. Or keep a stash of protein bars or water bottles in your car, and if you encounter a homeless person begging from a street corner, simply hand them food and water instead of cash. You're not handing it to the homeless guy—you're handing it to Jesus.

_____ *Check here when you have completed today's God Challenge.*

Notes

DAY NINETEEN

Unplugged

We pursue God because, and only because, He has first put an urge within us that spurs us to the pursuit.[37]

—A. W. TOZER

Most of us would say that deep inside, we long for a deeper relationship with God. We can ignore that desire very easily because our lives are so busy, and we have available to us so many enticing distractions. But when we stop for a moment, we realize how strange that feels—stopping. We quickly come face-to-face with our restlessness.

We are wired, in more ways than one. We seem never to be without electronic stimulation. We're connected by cell phone or Blackberry to anyone who wants to demand our attention. We've got portable entertainment constantly available to us on our iPod, iTouch, iPhone, iPad. I-this, I-that. *Ai-yi-yi!*

In the midst of all this electronic stimulation, God invites us to literally unplug. And if we are honest, something deep in our soul longs to have a deeper experience of God. As Tozer and other authors have wisely pointed out, that desire is put within us by God himself—what we think is *our* desire for God is actually God's initiative, God wanting us.

What we don't realize is that all the wires (or even wireless) we've tangled ourselves in prevent us from experiencing him fully. Even in times of solitude, we bring along our MP3 players, albeit loaded with Christian music. Music has its place; worship can help us to connect with God, but there is a deeper place that we can go if we are quiet enough to hear the "still, small voice" that is often blocked out by the noise of our daily lives. *If we are willing to completely unplug from everything else, we can connect with God.*

Completely? Can you imagine it? What if you could be alone with God for a while? Alone and unplugged: no phone or e-mail (because that equals bringing people and their demands with you), no books or movies (other people's ideas), no music or even recorded sermons (distractions). This is about you and silence and your deep desire for God's presence, which can feel very raw and a bit frightening at first. What would happen if you spent a bit of time with God, alone and utterly quiet? Just you and God and no one else—no machinery or distractions.

I assume you've picked up this book because you want to grow spiritually. You want to experience the presence of God more deeply, more authentically. The part of you that connects with God is your soul. And that may sound sentimental, but it's actually the truest part of you. And it's a part that is both wild and shy, as Parker Palmer writes:

> The soul is like a wild animal . . . the last thing we should do is go crashing through the woods yelling for it to come out. But if we will walk quietly into the woods, sit patiently at the base of the tree, breathe with the earth, and fade into our surroundings, the wild creature we seek might put in an appearance.[38]

These are things that you cannot learn by reading about them—they can only be understood by practicing them. It will take discipline and perseverance to find a way to be alone, but what you will experience in that place is something no words can fully describe.

Spiritual director and author Ruth Barton writes, "There is little in Western culture that supports us in entering into what feels like unproductive time for being (beyond human effort) and listening (beyond human thought)."[39]

🌲 TODAY'S CHALLENGE

Take a look at your calendar for today. Likely it is crowded with appointments and obligations. However, if you are honest, you'll see that you have unscheduled blocks of time—perhaps the time after supper when you zone out in front of the TV, or time you spend commuting. Or the time that disappears while you're on Facebook. Can you find, in today or tomorrow's schedule, an hour to be alone with God? You'll have to consider it an appointment—one that cannot be broken or postponed. Don't put it off until next week—make it happen either today or tomorrow. If someone calls and wants your time, tell them you have a prior commitment. You don't have to tell them that you have a meeting with the Creator of the Universe.

Your challenge today is to be alone for an hour, only present with God. Do not bring books, worship music, or any electronic stuff. Turn off your phone. Begin by simply being quiet, letting go of all the thoughts that jump through your mind. Ask God to be with you, to make his presence known to you.

It may help to imagine Jesus sitting beside you, asking you very gently, "What do you need?" Let your soul answer this question without editing. Have a conversation with Jesus about your needs, about your desire to know him more deeply. Simply rest in his presence; allow yourself to experience his love. Only when we stop performing, stop running, stop accomplishing, at least for a little while, can we truly experience the unconditional love that God wants to give us.

____ *Check here when you have completed today's God Challenge.*

Notes

Conquerors

*Be kind, for everyone you meet is
fighting a great battle.*

—ATTRIBUTED TO BOTH PHILO
OF ALEXANDRIA AND PLATO

Just making it through the day is sometimes a struggle. Jesus'
observation that "in this world you will have trouble" (John
16:33) is a spot-on description of our experience. We grow
weary and tired. Our lives feel like those credit card commercials where the hordes of barbarians are about to come crashing
through the door.

Our jobs are hard, our families have many needs, and we're
supposed to help out at church and coach our kids' soccer
teams. I remember one time when I was writing a manuscript
full-time, putting together a newsletter part-time, doing some
conference speaking, serving on the preaching team at church,

coaching both my girls' teams, and trying to keep up with my son's school activities—in addition to the usual blend of mowing the yard, being a husband and father, and trying to keep some food on the table. Everyone seems to want more of our time and energy than is possible to give. We battle fear and discouragement.

When we face struggles of all kinds, the Bible tells us to rejoice (see James 1:2). However, that's not as counterintuitive as you may think. We don't necessarily rejoice because of the trials, but because of the presence of God with us. We can celebrate the good news that God is with us in the midst of our troubles.

Of course, you're reading this book because you want to experience that presence more deeply—you want to grow closer to God. In the battles of life, you want to know that he's with you, helping you—not out of obligation, but because he genuinely cares about you.

And he does. But how can we keep that in mind while dodging the flaming arrows that seem to come our way?

Memorizing Scripture is a spiritual discipline that will help us to feel God's presence more deeply. When you memorize, you essentially make God's thoughts (as expressed in the pages of Scripture) your thoughts. You replace your discouraged or uncertain thoughts with thoughts of courage and love.

Rather than seeing this as one more thing you have to do, think of it as equipping yourself to do all the other things on your to-do list better.

Our feelings can be deeply influenced by our thoughts. While we can't choose our feelings, we can choose to think about certain things. As Paul wrote, "Whatever is true, whatever is noble, whatever is right . . . *think* about such things"

(Philippians 4:8). Why would he tell us to think about good, lovely, true things? Why not just say "be" these things—be good, be noble, be true? Because how we behave flows out of how we feel, and how we feel flows out of how we think. And it's much easier to change the way you think than to change the way you behave. Behavior that's transformed by changed thinking is more likely to stay transformed.

The Bible never denies the struggle; it simply gives us weapons with which to fight. The whole of Romans 8 talks about the struggles we face, and how we can overcome them:

> Who shall separate us from the love of Christ? Shall trouble or hardship or persecution or famine or nakedness or danger or sword? As it is written:
>   "For your sake we face death all day long;
>   we are considered as sheep to be slaughtered."
>
> vv. 35–36

Paul goes on to answer his own question in this way:

> No, in all these things we are more than conquerors through him who loved us. For I am convinced that neither death nor life, neither angels nor demons, neither the present nor the future, nor any powers, neither height nor depth, nor anything else in all creation, will be able to separate us from the love of God that is in Christ Jesus our Lord.
>
> vv. 37–39

God is reminding us that if we are connected to him, to his love, through Jesus, we can handle anything. We are more than conquerors.

Sometimes life does not feel like a battle, but more like drudgery. In fact, a battle might be nice because it wouldn't be so boring. In some ways, this very typical feeling is a battle as well—a battle we are losing because we have given up. God calls us to live our lives as an adventure with him.

And both feeling overwhelmed and feeling bored come from our thinking. So we need to replace those thoughts with God's truth. We can do so by memorizing Scripture.

☘ Today's Challenge

Today, you can change your thinking by replacing whatever thoughts of defeat or exhaustion you may have with some important truth from the book of Romans.

Your challenge today is to memorize Romans 8:37–39. Begin by reading through the entire chapter of Romans 8, so that you have the context of this amazing promise from God. You can select whichever version you like (the passage above is from the New International Version). Some people find the King James Version easier to memorize because of the poetic rhythms of the old English. Others like the contemporary feel of the New Living Translation. Choose any version, but pick one and memorize these verses:

> In all these things we are more than conquerors through him that loved us. For I am persuaded, that neither death, nor life, nor angels, nor principalities, nor powers, nor things present, nor things to come, nor height, nor depth, nor any other creature, shall be able to separate us from the love of God, which is in Christ Jesus our Lord. (Romans 8:37–39 KJV)

When you face struggles, say the verses. Replace your negative thinking with truth from God's Word. You are more than a conqueror.

_____ *Check here when you have completed today's God Challenge.*

Notes

DAY TWENTY-ONE

Fruitful Living

Why should my heart be fixed where my home is not?
Heaven is my home; God in Christ is all my happiness:
and where my treasure is, there my heart should be.[40]

—MARGARET CHARLTON BAXTER

Congratulations! Now that you are halfway through a book on getting closer to God, you may want to stop and assess: How are you doing, spiritually speaking?

You may respond by saying, "Well, how would I know how I'm doing? How do I measure something as nebulous as spiritual growth?" In some seasons of life, we can feel like we are making progress, while in others, we may be discouraged. But often those seasons of discouragement are actually times of growth, because we are "right-sizing" our ego. We're realizing we are not perfect, and that is a huge step of growth, even though the realization requires humility.

Various religions and denominations have used different benchmarks over the years to try to measure spiritual growth.

Some might measure it by how much money you donate, how regularly you show up in church, how many prayers you recite, how often you read your Bible (or how many chapters you read, or how early in the morning you read it). Others might look at rule-keeping—are you avoiding drinking, dancing, smoking? But one can keep outward rules without being inwardly transformed.

That is why the Bible provides different benchmarks: *God looks at the heart.* While it's important to go to church, to be generous, to read the Bible and behave decently, it is possible to do all of those things and remain virtually unchanged in your heart.

The Bible says that true growth results in the transformation of your character. Your character is your inner self, the person you are when no one's looking. And it says the character of a Christian is first and foremost marked by love. So are you becoming more loving? If so, you are growing in Christlikeness.

While the steps you have taken in this challenge are hopefully moving you toward God, your growth is not entirely up to you. In fact, the Bible says that when we seek after God, he responds by coming close to us and working in our lives. James 4:8 says, "Come near to God and he will come near to you." It is a relationship of mutuality and cooperation. We cannot do it alone, nor should we sit back passively and wait for God to change us. Jonathan Edwards said, "We are not merely passive, nor yet does God do some and we do the rest. But God does all, and we do all. God produces all, we act all. . . . God is the only proper author and fountain; we are only the proper actors. We are in different respects, wholly passive and wholly active." [41]

When we open ourselves to growth, God's Spirit works in our lives. The Bible says the product or result (the fruit) of God's Spirit in our lives is a change in our very nature: "But the Holy Spirit produces this kind of fruit in our lives: love, joy, peace, patience, kindness, goodness, faithfulness, gentleness, and self-control. There is no law against these things!" (Galatians 5:22–23 NLT).

Notice that the text does not say "fruits" as if there were many. The word is *fruit*, and the list that follows is a multifaceted description of that fruit, or "product," of the Spirit. As an apple tree produces apples, the Spirit produces people who are loving and kind and patient and joyful and peaceful. All these characteristics together describe what spiritual fruit looks like.

The spiritual practices you've been learning, and will continue to learn, will provide some space for God's Spirit to continue to cultivate that fruit. They open up space for the Spirit to work in our lives. The evidence of that work is the change in our character, which should transform the way we treat others, the way we think, and the way we act.

So how can you tell if you are growing? While the fruit of the Spirit is not a to-do list, it can be a helpful tool for self-inventory.

🌳 Today's Challenge

An important spiritual discipline that helps us grow is self-examination. Self-examination is a prayerful and honest inventory in which we ask God to show us how we are doing—where we are growing and where we need to grow.

Galatians 5:22–23 provides a helpful framework for the discipline of self-examination, so your practice for today is to read slowly through these verses and use them to do a spiritual inventory. Are you more loving than you were, say, six months ago? Are you more patient? Can you point to specific actions or attitudes you've had that would give evidence of that?

This is not meant to be an exercise in beating yourself up. All of us are sinners—and I certainly lead the pack. But if you find that you could stand some improvement, say, in patience, you can't do it by trying extra hard. You'll have to put yourself in situations where you are forced to be patient. For example, let others go ahead of you in line, or offer to baby-sit a two-year-old. These are ways to train yourself in patience.

Where have you seen growth in these nine areas of your life? Where do you need to grow? What are some specific practices that would help you to be kinder, gentler, more loving? Spend a few minutes and write down areas of your life you'd like to see slowly transformed.

_____ *Check here when you have completed today's God Challenge.*

Notes

Day Twenty-two

Forgiveness

If it is possible, as far as it depends on you, live at peace with everyone.

—Romans 12:18

One of the biggest barriers to spiritual growth is something you might not expect. It is not lack of Bible reading or prayer, or slacking off in church attendance. Rather, it is unresolved conflict.

Our relationship with God begins when we admit our need for forgiveness. We cannot earn God's favor; we must accept the free gift of his grace. We are sinners who are in need of a Savior.

If this is the foundation of our relationship with God, we must forgive others. And yet, people who claim to be saved by grace will walk around for years holding grudges. What's amazing is that they are perplexed by their lack of growth. They can't imagine why God seems so distant. They forget this basic truth: You cannot have it both ways, to live as one who is forgiven requires that you also forgive others.

The verse above reminds us that we should live at peace with everyone. This verse also acknowledges that sometimes relational breakdown is beyond our control. That's why it says, "as far as it depends on you." That means *you* make the effort to forgive, to restore community. *You* stay open to restoration.

Similarly, Hebrews 12:14 says, "Make every effort to live in peace with all men and to be holy; without holiness no one will see the Lord." Holiness means, in part, to love even those who don't deserve it. And that often requires that we extend forgiveness.

In Matthew 6, we read the famous prayer Jesus taught his disciples. But when we recite this prayer, we don't include the words Jesus said in the very next breath:

> *Forgive us our debts,*
>   *as we also have forgiven our debtors.*
> *And lead us not into temptation,*
>   *but deliver us from the evil one.*
>
> *For if you forgive men when they sin against you, your heav-*
>   *enly Father will also forgive you. But if you do not forgive*
>   *men their sins, your Father will not forgive your sins.*
>
> Matthew 6:12–15

The verse asking for God's help in resisting temptation is sandwiched between two verses about forgiveness. We often pray, "Lead us not into temptation" when facing the urge to lie, cheat, steal, or lust, but its place in the text tells us something important. When we are tempted not to forgive someone, do we ask God to help us? Do we even consider that holding a grudge is a sin? Or that unforgiveness is a temptation we need to ask God to help us resist?

And give attention to Jesus' words: "If you do not forgive [others] . . . your Father will not forgive [you]." This is not an isolated verse but a major theme in the Bible. When Peter asked

Jesus how many times he had to forgive, Jesus told him to keep on forgiving, and told him a parable about an unmerciful servant who eventually is punished with jail and torture because he would not forgive (see Matthew 18:21–35). It ends with this warning: "This is how my heavenly Father will treat each of you unless you forgive your brother from your heart."

Jesus said the most important commandments were to love God and love your neighbor. Those are two sides to the same coin. You can't love God without loving your neighbor. And you can't claim to love your neighbor if you haven't forgiven him.

Theologian Lew Smedes notes that when we forgive, we think we're letting the other person off the hook. Not so. We're letting ourselves off the hook. *When we forgive, we take away the power of the person who wronged us to keep on hurting us.*

"Forgiving is the only way to be fair to yourself," Smedes asserts.

> Would it be fair to you that the person who hurt you once goes on hurting you the rest of your life? When you refuse to forgive, you are giving the person who walloped you once the privilege of hurting you all over again—in your memory. Remember this: The first person to get the benefits of forgiving is the person who does the forgiving. . . . Forgiving is, first of all, a way of helping yourself to get free of the unfair pain somebody caused you.[42]

🌱 Today's Challenge

Forgiveness is not an optional part of the Christian life.

Are you angry at someone? Someone who has wronged you in a terrible way? Are you continuing to let that person hurt you over and over again by replaying the situation in your mind, and refusing to forgive?

Forgiveness is a process, and something you have to want to do. You cannot just say, "I forgive you." You have to mean it. There's an emotional part of the decision that goes beyond words—and it can take some time. So your challenge today is to move toward forgiveness. Ask God to give you the desire to forgive the person who wronged you.

You may say that you'd forgive if the other person would only apologize. But true forgiveness does not require repentance or apology on the other person's part. It is merely a decision you make to stop allowing the other person to go on hurting you.

There's a huge difference between forgiveness and reconciliation. If someone is abusive to you or has betrayed you, you can forgive that person without restoring the relationship. In fact, sometimes the only way to forgive is to get away from the person. Reconciliation requires both parties to repent, but forgiveness only requires one person to decide to forgive.

You may want to write a letter to the person who wronged you, explaining how you felt when she hurt you, but then telling her that you forgive her. You can either send the letter, or burn it as a symbol of letting go of the hurt. But start right now. Who do you need to forgive?

_____ *Check here when you have completed today's God Challenge.*

Notes

_____

_____

_____

_____

Day Twenty-three
All's Well

There is no such thing as sad adoration or unhappy praise.[43]

—John Piper

Do you go to a hymnbook church, or a projector church? Do you sing choruses or hymns? Are the songs you sing mostly from this century, or mostly from a few centuries ago?

I'm frankly not interested in the debate about which of these worship styles is superior. Whether or not you are familiar with the classic hymns of the Protestant tradition, many of them express theology and truth in beautiful and poetic language. One hymn worth learning is "It Is Well With My Soul." The words are beautiful and stirring, but the backstory is even more inspiring.

This well-loved hymn opens with these courageous words:

> When peace like a river attendeth my way,
> When sorrows like sea billows roll;
> Whatever my lot, Thou has taught me to say,
> "It is well, it is well with my soul."

The hymn was written in 1873 by Horatio G. Spafford. This man was a successful lawyer from Chicago and a friend and well-known supporter of the great evangelist Dwight L. Moody. The words were written at a time when, from all external appearances, Spafford's life was not going well.

Only a few years before, he had lost a good portion of his wealth when several buildings he owned on Chicago's Lake Michigan shore were destroyed in the Great Chicago Fire. Looking for a reprieve from the struggles, he decided to take his wife and four daughters on vacation to England. There they could rest, he thought, and also join Moody's current evangelistic campaign.

The day the family was to sail from New York to Europe on the French steamer *Ville de Havre,* a last-minute crisis arose with Spafford's business dealings, forcing him to stay in America. Rather than delay their holiday, Spafford sent his family on without him and returned to Chicago. Nine days later, he received a telegram from his wife. It began: "Saved Alone." Their four daughters had drowned when the *Ville de Havre* collided with another ship and sank instantly.

Spafford quickly returned to New York and sailed to meet his devastated wife, who only escaped drowning because a board happened to float up under her unconscious body.

As he crossed the Atlantic, the ship's captain told him when they were passing the spot where his daughters had drowned. Spafford, the story goes, went to his stateroom and wrote the hymn. The words "it is well" come from 2 Kings 4:26, where a mother who has lost her only child also declares, "It is well" (KJV).

One of the most important questions we can ask as we try to grow in our relationship with God is, "Do I trust God?" Do I believe he has my best interests at heart, even when things go badly? Am I still a friend to God even in times of struggle, or when he disappoints me?

Do you love God even in times of loss? In those seasons when his protection seems to have been withdrawn from your life? Can you praise him not because of your circumstances, but in spite of them? *Part of growing closer to God is learning how to love him more than you love his blessings.*

It's not easy to do. Meditating on this hymn and its history may help you step toward loving God unconditionally.

🌳 TODAY'S CHALLENGE

Two stories in the Gospels (both are told in more than one gospel) are set in a boat on a lake during a storm. In one story, Jesus is with his disciples, but taking a nap. He wakes up and rebukes the wind, and all is still. In the other, Jesus sends his disciples out in a boat and ends up walking on the lake to them—again during a storm.

The storms of life are no match for the power of God. He doesn't keep the storms from coming. And in fact, in the second story referenced above, you could argue that Jesus knowingly sent his disciples into a storm, while he stayed behind for a little quiet time. Storms happen, but God's power is always greater, and storms actually provide an opportunity for God to display his power. The question is not whether your life will have storms, but whether those storms will be an opportunity for you to allow God to display his power through your life.

Go to a Web site like *www.biblestudycharts.com/A_Daily_ Hymn.html* where you can find the lyrics and hear the melody of "It Is Well With My Soul" and read Horatio Spafford's story in more detail. Use an online search engine to find a recording of it being sung. Your challenge today is to meditate on all six verses of this hymn.

The words may seem old-fashioned to you, but they convey great truth. Even during storms, we can say, "It is well." Why? One verse gives the reason: "My sin, not in part but the whole, is nailed to His cross and I bear it no more!" This is what makes us able to say, "It is well." Knowing that we have been saved from sin and death, we no longer need to be afraid of life's challenges, or even tragedies. We know the outcome and we know who controls the wind and waves in life. Read those verses; then remind yourself that God is greater than your circumstances.

_____ *Check here when you have completed today's God Challenge.*

Notes

Eating With Sinners

*Being an extrovert isn't essential to evangelism—
obedience and love are.*[44]

—REBECCA MANLEY PIPPERT

When Jesus came to earth, he chose to surround himself with a group of disciples who became his closest friends. But keep in mind that when Jesus first met them, many were not necessarily the religious type.

As did most rabbis of his day, Jesus taught in synagogues and as an itinerant preacher, but also in the more intimate setting of his small group of followers. As they walked along with Christ, they might see someone out planting in a field. Jesus would use that moment to say something like, "The kingdom of God is like a seed." Their conversations are not all recorded for us in Scripture, but I imagine the disciples would ask Jesus a bunch of questions about the things he said.

Jesus' disciples were not the religious elite. Rather, they were simple fishermen and blue-collar workers. Matthew had been a tax collector—despised by his fellow Jews because he collected Roman taxes from them, and because the profession was known for its corruption. But Jesus saw something in Matthew—that his job did not wholly define him. So Christ invited Matthew to follow him, and Matthew did. He left a lucrative career to become a disciple of a rabbi.

While Matthew left his career, he did not leave his friends. And some of his friends were, well, a little rough around the edges. The Bible describes them as "tax collectors and 'sinners.'" Right after Matthew said yes to Jesus, he invited Jesus over to dinner so that he and the other disciples could meet Matthew's friends:

> While Jesus was having dinner at Matthew's house, many tax collectors and "sinners" came and ate with him and his disciples. When the Pharisees saw this, they asked his disciples, "Why does your teacher eat with tax collectors and 'sinners'?" On hearing this, Jesus said, "It is not the healthy who need a doctor, but the sick. But go and learn what this means: 'I desire mercy, not sacrifice.' For I have not come to call the righteous, but sinners."
>
> MATTHEW 9:10–13

In the ancient Middle East, to eat with someone was "to extend an honor, an offering of peace, trust, and forgiveness," authors Ann Spangler and Lois Tverberg note. "To be a guest at a family's table meant that you were under their protection. As long as you were with the family, they were honor-bound to defend you, even at the cost of their lives."[45]

Matthew knew something had changed in his heart, but it was still new to him. Maybe he tried to explain it to his friends—but found they still had questions. So he tried another strategy: he simply invited them all to dinner. Unlike other parties at Matthew's house, this one included Jesus and the other disciples. Perhaps Matthew was hoping that his friends would understand, after some conversation with Jesus, why Matthew had made this radical change in his life. Maybe he hoped they'd be inspired to make some changes in their own lives.

Jesus gladly rubbed shoulders with people who needed God. Most rabbis went out of their way to avoid the contamination of "unclean" people, but Jesus seemed to go looking for them. Spangler and Tverberg note that the Pharisees didn't realize "that Jesus was living out his own parable, playing the role of the forgiving father welcoming home the prodigal. . . . Each time Jesus ate with sinners, he was revealing the kingdom of God." [46]

How can we imitate this particular aspect of Jesus' character? How can we follow his willingness to spend time with and love those who are far from God? How can we, when we eat with "sinners," reveal the kingdom of God?

Some Christians avoid hanging around with unbelievers because they fear they might be a bad influence. Especially if you came to faith as an adult, you may think you need to leave your old life behind and only associate with other Christians.

The question we must ask is: *Are you an influencer, or one who is influenced?* Do you think Jesus was tempted to become a sinner when he hung around with tax collectors? No. He didn't see their lifestyle as fun—he simply saw human beings who needed God's love. One way we express our love of God and our love of others is to tell people about God.

Do you have friends who are unbelievers? Or are all of your friends Christians? If you have friends who do not share your beliefs, do they know about your faith? One of the surest ways to grow stronger spiritually is to share our faith with others. But that's hard to do unless you have friends who do not yet know Jesus.

Conversations about spiritual things, especially with people who don't believe the same things you do, can be difficult—but they will stretch and grow your faith. It's one thing to simply say you believe something. But when you have to articulate the reasons why you believe it, your faith goes to a deeper level.

🌳 TODAY'S CHALLENGE

How can you follow Jesus' example of sharing fellowship with unbelievers? One good way to start is to follow Matthew's example, and *throw a party*.

Some people are more gifted in evangelism than others. Some Christians naturally exude God's love in a contagious way. If this is not you (yet), that's okay.

Today, pray for an unbeliever that you know. Pray for her specific needs, but also for an opportunity to share your faith with her.

Then plan a dinner party, like Matthew did. Invite a few unbelieving friends and a few Christians—especially those who are good at talking about their faith. Pray for conversations that will happen as people enjoy a meal together. Don't think of this as a time to evangelize, but rather as a time to simply share your life with other people.

____ *Check here when you have completed today's God Challenge.*

Notes

_____
_____
_____
_____
_____

Why I Love You

> In one hand I hold the truth of God's vastness, and in
> the other hand I hold the truth of God's desire for in-
> timacy. . . . God's infinite greatness, which we would
> expect to diminish us, actually makes possible the very
> closeness that we desire.[47]
>
> —PHILIP YANCEY

A friend of mine has an annual tradition with her two young
sons. On their birthdays, she writes a list entitled "Ten Things
I Like About You" for each of them. She then creates a list of
each boy's strengths. She praises them for being kind, for their
creativity, for their abilities in school or athletics, or whatever
character qualities or skills she's noticed them developing. She
tries to focus on their character, and to name integrity and godliness when she sees it in their lives.

The boys of course treasure their lists, even though they, being
boys, don't get very mushy about it. But if she ever tries to skip
this annual exercise, they complain loudly until she completes it.

While God is not dependent upon our praise in the way a child is with his parents, God still loves to hear from us. In the same way parents love to hear "I love you" from their children, God loves to hear praise from us. And just as we would rather hear specifics than a vague "You're terrific," I think God loves to hear specific praises from us. It lets him know we're paying attention.

When we praise God, when we honor him, it is not only for his sake. *The discipline of honoring God changes our hearts.* We become more grateful people simply by expressing gratitude. We become more positive simply by naming positive things in our lives—including the abundant blessings of God. We become more humble as we remember that we need him and that his love for us is unconditional.

Praising God is also an important spiritual discipline because it reminds us that *the good things in our lives are not merely the result of our own efforts and hard work.* Even if we work hard in order to have material things, God has given us the brains or brawn to be able to do our job, and the blessing of employment. His goodness is the ultimate source of all that is good in our lives.

To tell God what we love about him is to worship him. To worship is to honor and adore—to name the value of something. While God is really the only one worthy of worship, we often unwittingly worship other people or things. Adele Calhoun writes:

> *Worship* is a word most often associated with religion. But worship can be found in the lives of secularists, agnostics and even atheists. The simple truth is that everybody looks to something or someone to give their lives meaning. Worship reveals the somethings or someones we value most. What we love and adore and focus on forms us into the people we become.[48]

Worship—whether we worship money, success, or God—forms us. That is why worship of God is so essential a practice for spiritual formation. When we think about God and appreciate who he is and what he's done, it transforms our hearts.

🌳 Today's Challenge

In previous chapters, we've looked at the psalms, which take us to school, so to speak, on praising God. They are helpful in teaching us to pray prayers of praise. So as you take on today's challenge, you may want to read a few psalms. I've found Psalms 18, 66, 72, 86, and 107 are good examples, because they talk about praising God for his great deeds.

What has God done in your life? How has he helped you? How has he changed you? What specific blessings have you received that made you simply shake your head and say, "Wow! Only God could do this."

Today, take some time to think about God and what he has done for you. How has he blessed you? What good gifts—whether things, people, circumstances—has he provided?

Then, think about *who* he is. You know you appreciate friends who love you not for what you do for them, but because of who you are. God also deserves our love and admiration, not because of what he can do for us, but because of who he is—amazing and powerful and loving and good.

Now take some time to praise him for all of those things—for how he's blessed you, and for who he is. Write it down. You don't need to write a psalm if you don't want to, but make a list of at least twenty reasons why you love God. Thank him for material blessings, but move on to relational blessings and the ways he has formed your character. Include some attributes of God—perhaps you love him because he is righteous, because he is loving, because he cared enough to send his Son.

Finally, take some time to pray this list to God, telling him that you love him, naming specific reasons why you appreciate him. What a wonderful way to remind ourselves of our great God.

_____ *Check here when you have completed today's God Challenge.*

Notes

Day Twenty-six

Take and Read

*The man who does not read good books has no advantage
over the man who can't read them.*[49]

—Mark Twain

I learned to read before I started school, probably because both my parents were dedicated readers. Neither of them had more than an eighth-grade education, but both were very intelligent. There's a difference between being stupid and being uneducated. My parents were smart and taught me the value of reading. My father explained to me why Mark Twain was the greatest writer of all time, and why it was important to read the newspaper. I loved nautical fiction because he did, and I loved mysteries because my mom did.

So in first grade, I chattered a lot to my teacher about the books I was reading. I probably asked her what she was reading, and in response to my talking about books, one day she explained to us how books were made—how an idea became a manuscript, then was edited and printed and bound. I was fascinated.

That day, I walked into the house after school and proudly announced to my mother, "When I grow up, I'm going to be a book guy!"

I was six years old. And that's pretty much what I ended up doing—being a "book guy." I've made my living as a writer, editor, publisher, or literary agent for decades now. I love books. I suppose I love all the arts, but a book will shape your life far more than a movie or a song or a painting ever will. While books cannot solve all your problems, they can offer helpful information for moving forward from a lot of them.

An unavoidable truth about the Christian life is that no one can do it for you, but you can find truth that will help you grow. Many people hop from church to church, or small group to small group, looking to get "spiritually fed." The truth is, while churches and small groups can provide some spiritual nourishment, you won't get far if you're only spoon-fed by someone else. *By reading good books, you can engage your mind and begin to feed yourself.*

Books can offer information, advice, and truth to help you in your growth as a person. They can remind you of the lessons of history and give you a big-picture perspective on politics, business, or war and peace. They can weave stories that, though fictional, tell great truths about people, relationships, or any number of subjects. Books can offer us an escape from our everyday problems, whether by offering sound advice, or by simply taking us to another place through story.

Anne Lamott's observations resonate deeply with me:

> What a miracle it is that out of these small, flat, rigid squares of paper unfolds world after world after world, worlds that sing to you, comfort and quiet or excite you. Books help us understand who we are and how we are to behave. They show us what community and friendship mean; they show us how to live and die.[50]

We are fortunate to live in a country of great publishing freedom. While that freedom sometimes gets abused and trash gets published, the flip side remains worthwhile—writers have freedom to write about the specifics of the Christian faith and how that faith applies to specific situations.

As you have embarked on this challenge to get closer to God, perhaps growth issues have risen to the surface of your life. Maybe you're realizing that you need some additional resources. For example, maybe you want to take your prayer life to a deeper level. Richard Foster, Walter Wangerin, and Philip Yancey have each written excellent books on prayer. Perhaps you struggle with doubt—John Ortberg's book *Faith and Doubt* can help you to see that doubt is a normal part of faith. Or Lee Strobel's *The Case for Christ* will show you the evidence for believing in Jesus. If you are looking for guidance, pick up *Hearing God* by Dallas Willard. If you're always worried, perhaps you'll want to read Max Lucado's *Fearless*.

Maybe you wrestle with materialism. A great way to loosen its grip on your life is to read a book on simplicity. Or maybe you feel stirred to do something to help the poor: Read Shane Claiborne or John Perkins or Lisa Samson. Maybe reading this book has gotten you interested in specific disciplines, such as solitude, fasting, or study. You can find books on any of those topics and dive in deeper.

✤ Today's Challenge

Imagine that you have joined a gym and signed up for a session with a personal trainer. Before the trainer can give you some exercises to improve your fitness, he's got to assess your strengths. He may have you do some simple tests to measure your strength, endurance, balance, or flexibility. That way he can recommend certain exercises to help you become more fit, whether you need to lift weights, do some cardio conditioning, or stretching.

In the same way, if we want to improve ourselves spiritually, we need to begin with self-assessment. Which areas of our spiritual lives are we doing well in, and which ones need improvement?

Spend a little time in prayer today, asking yourself this question: How am I doing spiritually? What issues are tripping me up? Which specific areas of my Christian life need a boost? Do I wrestle with worry or doubt? Am I in a season of grieving or sadness? Are my relationships healthy? Am I battling addictions (and perhaps in denial about them)? This is meant to be an honest self-assessment, so that you know where to concentrate.

Then visit a Christian bookstore or the inspirational section of a general bookstore. Find a book that speaks to your particular spiritual situation right now (worry, difficulty in prayer, grieving, needing an energy boost in your faith, etc.). Ask the staff—often they've read many of the books they sell.

When you find a book that addresses your particular situation, buy it and read it. This will likely take you more than one day—but start the process today.

_____ *Check here when you have completed today's God Challenge.*

Notes

Life . . . Interrupted

The genuine work of love is always a hidden work.[51]
—DIETRICH BONHOEFFER

If you want to grow closer to God, you cannot focus only on what you believe, on what truths you claim, or what you say you know. You must also act on your beliefs. How you live matters as much as what you claim to believe.

Is service a regular spiritual practice in your life? Perhaps you volunteer in your church or your community—leading a small group or serving as an usher at worship services. I used to volunteer once a week to teach English to new immigrants. As I mentioned in an earlier chapter, when I was in seminary, I led a regular church service in a nursing home. Over the years, I've volunteered in various ways.

This type of service is good, helpful, and stretching at times. I grew in kindness and patience as a result of doing it. It was a discipline that helped others as well, but I did it on my schedule.

What would happen to your spiritual growth if you took this to the next level? Instead of serving once a week on a day that suits you, what would happen if you began to see yourself as someone who simply serves as opportunities arise around you? What if you engaged in the ministry of interruption?

Jesus was often interrupted. On the way to help one person, someone else would come up and ask a question or beg for healing (see Luke 8:40–50). He'd be eating dinner, and a woman would fall at his feet crying (see Luke 7:36ff.). He tried to get alone to pray, and the disciples would come looking for him (see Mark 1:35ff.). Jesus never seemed bothered by these disturbances. Instead, he saw interruptions as opportunities for ministry.

Instead of seeing interruptions as a problem, what if we tried to see them as Jesus did: as an opportunity to serve? This is a test for our motives—a service that we don't sign up for and no one really notices, except the person we're serving.

In his classic book on Christian growth, *The Cost of Discipleship,* Dietrich Bonhoeffer wrote about the paradox between two commands that Jesus gives regarding service. In the Sermon on the Mount, he tells his followers to let their light shine, so that others may see their good deeds (Matthew 5:16). But in that same sermon, in Matthew 6:1, he tells them not to do acts of righteousness before men in order to be seen.

Bonhoeffer offers this explanation:

How is this paradox to be resolved? The first question to ask is: From whom are we to hide the visibility of our discipleship? Certainly not from other men, for we are told to let them see our light. No. We are to hide it from *ourselves.* Our task is simply to keep on following, looking only to our Leader who goes on before, taking no notice of ourselves or of what we are doing.[52]

This, Bonhoeffer argued, was what it meant to be obedient to God.

While we are to do good works, those works are not to be done so that others will praise us, but so that our works will *point others toward God.* When we serve others in his name, and point them toward him, we grow closer to God ourselves.

🌳 TODAY'S CHALLENGE

John Ortberg writes about "the ministry of being interrupted," in which God asks us to serve whomever he brings across our path:

> Sometimes in our work we must be interruptible for tasks that are not on our agenda. Sometimes we must live with the "latch off the door." Sometimes we need to be available to talk or pray with troubled people—people whom we will not be able to "cure" and who can't contribute to our career success.[53]

Ortberg writes that he sometimes sets aside a day to simply serve his family. "The idea is that when my only task is to be available, it is impossible to be interrupted. The goal of the day is simply to serve. But it is always humbling to see how quickly my need to create my own personal agenda arises."[54]

Today, your challenge is simply to be open to serving others, not on your timetable but theirs. Engage in the ministry of interruptions. Whether at home or at work, be willing to see interruptions as opportunities to serve others. When you are interrupted, put aside what you are doing to help or listen. Consider it your secret mission to serve your family or co-workers on this day. Don't tell anyone what you are doing, just serve them joyfully!

Throughout your day, ask God to show you whom you should serve. He may simply bring people across your path, or he may bring people to mind to pray for or get in touch with. But look for interruptions in your day. And imagine that what you are doing for others you are doing for Jesus.

_____ *Check here when you have completed today's God Challenge.*

Notes

Day Twenty-eight

Do You Trust?

Unwavering trust is a rare and precious thing because it often demands a degree of courage that borders on the heroic.[55]

—Brennan Manning

Do you worry? Or are you more of a laid-back, "it will all work out" type of person? Did you know that scientists have isolated a gene in the human DNA that they believe makes you more prone to be a worrier? (Are you worried right now that you have that gene?)

I'm not much of a worrier, but in our crazy world, worry seems almost inevitable. Our culture is designed for worry—every news report of a missing child or the latest ingredient that's found to cause cancer fills us with dread. As if the news weren't enough, we watch movies or television shows that spin stories on worst-case scenarios, and call scaring ourselves to death entertainment.

Worry is based on fear—fear that something bad will happen, that we won't get what we want, or that we'll get something we don't want. We worry about our jobs: whether we'll keep our job, find another job, or that we'll be stuck in the same job for years. We worry about our families: Will our kids be safe? Will our parents, as they get older, have adequate care? Will the burden of that care fall on us? We worry about money: if we have some we worry about losing it, and if we don't, we worry we'll never have enough. We worry about countless possible affronts to our health and safety.

Worry is like a disease that slowly tears us to pieces inside. We usually worry about things that are beyond our control—because the things that are within our control we can simply do something about. But our worry won't change anything, which is why worry is so counterproductive. It saps our energy without producing any change.

Jesus directly commanded his followers: *"Do not worry."* (See Matthew 6:25–34.) This wonderful passage on trusting God ends with this exhortation straight from Jesus: "Therefore do not worry about tomorrow, for tomorrow will worry about itself. Each day has enough trouble of its own."

Jesus also told his followers: "Do not be afraid." (See Mark 5:36; 6:50; Luke 1:13; 1:30, etc.) Over and over, he repeated this refrain, which is the most oft-repeated command through all of Scripture. If we are not afraid, then we won't worry.

How can we let go of worry? We need to remember that our feelings (such as fear) flow out of our thoughts (like worry). If I tell you, "Don't worry," you'll probably still worry because I haven't given you anything else to do. But do you realize what worry's opposite is? *Trust.* To defeat worry, we must choose to trust. *Trust is not based on our circumstances, but rather on our decision to believe God is in control.* Often we must trust in spite of our circumstances. When we choose to think thoughts of trust, the feeling that flows from that is peace. And, sometimes, courage.

Manning's quote, above, says we need courage in order to trust. This is true, but when we have an ounce of courage, and choose to trust, God gives us more courage in response to that trust. We feel braver when we choose to take God at his Word.

Jesus said, "Do not let your hearts be troubled. Trust in God; trust also in me" (John 14:1). The question is not "Can you make yourself stop worrying?" Rather, the question is, "Do you trust God?"

🌿 TODAY'S CHALLENGE

How can you build trust? Often the only way to build trust is to take a risk. It is one thing to say that God is trustworthy— but unless we actually trust him, our faith is mere hypothesis. We must take the risk of trusting God. That is the only path to freedom from worry.

Larry Crabb writes about the "cliff of safety," where we stand saying we trust God. But we never jump from the cliff and trust that his love will hold us. The only way to really develop trust is to be willing to step off the cliff and allow the rope of God's love to be tested.

Today, choose not to worry about anything. When something troubling arises, quickly commit it to God and then either (a) do something about it right away, or (b) realize the situation is beyond your control, so set it aside and move on to something else.

Write the following verses on an index card or sticky note, and put it somewhere you can see it during the day:

But strive first for the kingdom of God and his righteousness, and all these things will be given to you as well. So do not worry about tomorrow, for tomorrow will bring worries of its own. Today's trouble is enough for today.

MATTHEW 6:33–34 NRSV

Paul was a guy who had a lot to worry about, but he wrote these words to one of his protégés: "I am not ashamed, for I know the one in whom I have put my trust, and I am sure that he is able to guard until that day what I have entrusted to him" (2 Timothy 1:12 NRSV).

_____ *Check here when you have completed today's God Challenge.*

Notes

Day Twenty-nine

'Fess Up

*Confession is a difficult Discipline for us because
we all too often view the believing community as a
fellowship of saints before we see it as a fellowship
of sinners.*[56]

RICHARD FOSTER

It takes strength to do the right thing, to live according to God's
way, to make moral choices at work, at home, in our friendships.
But it takes even more strength and courage to admit it when
we have dropped the ball and made bad choices.

We try to put a spin on our bad behavior—but this is cow-
ardly, plain and simple. It takes true courage to admit when we
screw up. It takes even more courage to say "I'm sorry" when
our mistakes hurt the people around us. But in order to get free
of it, we have to first own it.

We have to remember that even when we have made mistakes, or outright rebelled against God, he still accepts us and loves us unconditionally. This does not mean he winks at our sin or shoves it under the rug. The Bible says, "If we confess our sins, he is faithful and just and will forgive us our sins and purify us from all unrighteousness" (1 John 1:9). Notice that important word at the beginning of the verse: *IF. If we confess.* The way to make things right with God is to confess.

We sometimes don't like the word *sin.* It makes us uncomfortable. In the Bible's original Greek, the word for sin is *hamartia.* This word, which came from language used by archers, means "a missing of the mark." When we sin, we miss the target of God's righteousness. But the word goes deeper than the archery analogy—because sin hurts our relationship with God, and with others. The good news is, sincere confession can change and heal those relationships.

Adele Calhoun writes: "Every time we confess how we have missed the mark of God's love and truth, we open ourselves up to the mending work of the cross. Jesus' wounds hold true life-changing power. This is the shocking reality that confession can open up to us."[57]

Sometimes I do hurtful or stupid things and don't realize how much I've missed the mark. I think I'm hitting bull's-eyes, when in fact I'm completely missing the target. Other times I simply choose to do wrong. I know it is sin, and I choose to do it anyway. That's when I have to have the guts to do some honest self-assessment and ask God, "How am I doing?"

King David, a biblical hero who loved God but was certainly not immune to sin (he committed adultery and murder in the same month), was called "a man after [God's] own heart" (see 1 Samuel 13:14), and he once wrote these words:

Search me, O God, and know my heart;
test me and know my thoughts.
See if there is any wicked way in me,
and lead me in the way everlasting.

Psalm 139:23–24 NRSV

These verses give us a model of prayer for self-examination, which is an essential step before confession. Have you ever had someone wrong you, and then apologize, but the apology feels cheap and insincere? That happens because the person really doesn't understand how much they hurt you, or what they did wrong. Sincere apology happens when you fully grasp exactly how badly you messed up.

In order to be in right relationship with God, we have to make it a practice to examine our conscience and compare our behavior to God's standards. Now, let me be clear: Nothing you've ever done or will do can separate you from God's love. He loves us in spite of our sin. We can't make him love us any less or any more. But he wants us to grow, and that means getting honest, and being humble.

🌱 TODAY'S CHALLENGE

Is there any "wicked way" in you? Spend a few minutes thinking about that. It may be that several things come to mind right away. Don't hurry through this process. Know that you are totally accepted and loved, even as you tell God about what you've done. If nothing comes to mind, sit and think for a few more minutes.

If you find that you're patting yourself on the back, thinking you've kept your nose pretty clean, take it to a deeper level. Take a look at Exodus 20:1–17, and read slowly through the Ten Commandments. Have you kept them? For example, number one is "You shall have no other gods before me." Would people looking at your life know that God comes first, that nothing else comes "before him"? Or would they assume by your schedule and priorities that your career, saving for retirement, or even shopping for another must-have item is your god? Work your way through the list.

Another passage you can use in this way is Matthew 5:1–11, the Beatitudes. Or, as Marjorie Thompson suggests, go through a list of common sins and see if any apply to you: "selfishness, dishonesty, resentment, fear, jealousy, self-pity, greed, envy, and hatred. . . . Pride, lust, impatience, procrastination, irresponsibility, judgmentalism, and lack of faith . . ."[58]

Once you've established the fact that you've sinned, confess those sins to God. But don't stop with merely naming your sin. Sure, it feels good to get it off your chest, but take the next step—*ask him to forgive you.* Then believe and accept that he does. Believe that Jesus' work on the cross has got you covered, that all the stuff you confessed is now gone, as far as the east is from the west, because of him.

Richard Foster writes:

Without the cross the Discipline of confession would be only psychologically therapeutic. But it is so much more. It involves an objective change in our relationship with God and a subjective change in us. It is a means of healing and transforming the inner spirit.[59]

Thank Jesus for his forgiveness, and pray for help in living as someone who is forgiven, is loved, and starts each day with a clean slate and a pure heart.

_____ *Check here when you have completed today's God Challenge.*

Notes

Day Thirty

Simplicity

A pivotal paradox for us to understand is that simplicity is both a grace and a Discipline.[60]

—Richard Foster

You're reading this book because you want to grow, you want to move forward in your spiritual journey, and you want to get closer to God. Often, self-improvement means doing things differently. We usually do this by adding some activities to our lives. If you need to lose weight, you might resolve to exercise more. If you need to improve your mind, you read challenging books instead of *People* magazine.

There's nothing wrong with those types of goals. But "spiritual growth" is not exactly the same as "self-improvement." In my view, *self-improvement focuses on what you do, and spiritual growth is about who you are becoming.* What will help us grow spiritually is to stop doing so much, to prune rather than plant. That's because spiritual growth could be better described as God renovating your life rather than you trying to renovate it yourself.

In fact, all the spiritual practices you've learned in this book are not about "doing" in order to impress God. Rather, they are ways to create some space for God in your life—space to be *with* him, not to do things *for* him.

It's counterintuitive, but often the thing that keeps us stuck spiritually is the hectic, hurried pace of our lives, which sometimes includes all the religious activities we have crammed into our schedule. Often our busyness has to do with the fact that we are working too much. To unwind from the stress, we play hard on the weekends, but it makes us more stressed and busy.

Do people ever tell you, "Wow! You have a lot on your plate" or "Sounds like you're pretty busy!" Do you have a list of people you intend to spend time with, once things settle down? I have news for you: Things don't settle down. Not on their own. You've got choices to make, and they have spiritual significance. Hurry and busyness will injure your soul. Hurry isolates you and disconnects you from the life you really want to live.

The first step toward a deeper spiritual life is to take note of what *simplify* means. Our culture has created an industry out of simplifying without even noticing the irony. We pick up *Real Simple* magazine or watch a television show on simplifying and don't even notice all the ads for more STUFF that accompanies the advice.

We think that simplicity is the same thing as simplifying, or even organizing, but it's much more than that. Simplifying is something we do on the outside, but simplicity is something we do on the inside. It's really about our focus, our inner reality, and our priorities. We won't find it by organizing closets or cleaning out the garage. Despite the messages of our culture, you cannot buy simplicity at The Container Store.

Simplicity is a condition of the heart: As Christian philosopher and author Søren Kierkegaard so aptly said: "Purity of heart is to will one thing."[61]

Jesus said, "But seek first his kingdom and his righteousness, and all these things will be given to you as well" (Matthew 6:33). What things is Jesus referring to? All the material possessions we worry about. That's really a good working definition for simplicity—seeking God's kingdom first, and trusting that he'll take care of the rest. Simplicity is about a singular focus on God, and ordering our lives around that reality.

🌿 Today's Challenge

One year I gave up Facebook for Lent. I use Facebook to keep in touch with people I work with, to promote my business, and, well, also to waste some time. I could rationalize using it, but I gave it up for the forty-day period. I suddenly felt I had extra time on my hands. I was also able to focus more on my relationship with God. My life felt simpler, less scattered. My family also appreciated it!

Richard Foster writes: "Simplicity involves a consciously chosen course of action. . . . What we *do* does not give us simplicity, but it does put us in the place where we can receive it. . . . Simplicity is an inward reality that can be seen in an outward lifestyle."[62]

What are some things you could do to put yourself in a place to receive the grace of simplicity? Start by listing the activities that take up your time: work and family, obviously. Maybe you exercise or play a sport, or are a part of a small group, and those take time. But how much of your time gets eaten up by watching TV or surfing the Internet? Of these activities, which could you cut back on, or cut out completely, to simplify? While you can't quit your job, could you work fewer hours? If you typically work late every night, could you make it home for dinner a couple of times a week? Keep track (by writing it down) how many hours you spend on TV or the Internet—it's probably more than you realize. Could you trim some of that in order to get more time with God, with your family, or even to get more rest?

Depending on how long your list is, cut out two or more activities. Sometimes if you've made a commitment for a specific time (say, to taking a class or playing on a team), you have to honor that commitment. But when that obligation is over, don't replace it with another. Learn to say a spiritually freeing and God-honoring word: *no*.

Simplicity is also about being content. If we are content, we don't need as much stuff, or to replace our old stuff with new stuff quite so often. What are some things that you think you need to replace with the latest version? Your TV? Your computer? Your cell phone? Could you be content with the things you have? How might practicing contentment put you in the place to receive the grace of simplicity? Take a few minutes and decide on a couple of simple steps you could take to simplify your life.

_____ *Check here when you have completed today's God Challenge.*

Notes

DAY THIRTY-ONE

Practicing the Presence

We may ignore, but we can nowhere evade, the presence of God. The world is crowded with Him. He walks every-where incognito. And the incognito is not always hard to penetrate. The real labour is to remember, to attend. In fact, to come awake. Still more, to remain awake.[63]

—C. S. LEWIS

A few years ago, I moved to a small home near the Oregon coast, within walking distance of the beach. On a beautiful day recently, I made myself get up from my desk. I work from home, but that often means I end up working way too many hours. So I pushed away from the computer. I walked to the beach, then along the shore, enjoying the sunshine and sea gulls on a perfect summer day. I found a place to sit in the sand and watch the waves. I had no real agenda other than being thankful. After a while, I got up and walked home, more aware of God's presence than I had been earlier that day.

During that time of solitude, I didn't really bring petitions or concerns to God. I didn't confess any big sins or ask any big questions. While I often pray for God's help or intercede on someone's behalf, this was more of a chance to hang out with God, to spend some time in companionable silence, to simply be thankful for him and appreciate the beauty of his creation. And even as I went back to the computer and phone to continue working, I had a sense of God's presence. I didn't leave God sitting on the beach, of course. He's always with me—but that time helped remind me to be aware of that fact.

The Bible tells us to "pray without ceasing" (1 Thessalonians 5:17 NASB). This verse is not telling us to chatter incessantly, like an annoying child, at God. Prayer is not just speaking at God, but thinking about him, being aware of his presence, noticing the way he is working in the world around us. *Prayer is listening*—by reflecting on Scripture, by letting him speak to us, by letting him remind our hearts of his love for us. To pray without ceasing is to practice the presence of God, to keep reminding ourselves that he is around us, and that he loves us. It's like sitting with a friend you know well enough that words aren't essential.

The Bible tells us that God is everywhere—that he is omnipresent. But often we are moving too fast or are too distracted to notice him. We miss his joy in the smile of a friend or a stranger, and we miss the beauty he's created in our world.

As I said in a previous chapter, sometimes the greatest obstacle to our spiritual growth is our hectic, busy pace of life. *In order to connect with God, we need stillness and quiet.* We need to get away from the noise and confusion so that we can pay attention to what really matters, so that we can notice what God is doing and take the time to tell him we're grateful.

A monk named Brother Lawrence wrote centuries ago about "practicing the presence of God" by simply bringing God to mind as he went through his day. When he did simple chores in the monastery, whether it was peeling potatoes or scrubbing the floor, he would turn his attention to God. It didn't take a lot of effort. When his thoughts would stray, he'd gently steer them back to God, often by way of thinking of things he was grateful for. He'd imagine that as he worked, God was sitting beside him, being with him. He found he could tune in to God's voice through this practice, and had an increasing awareness of God's very real presence.

We often compartmentalize our lives—we have time for God when we go to church, or for a few minutes when we have a quiet time or devotions in the morning, but not during the busyness of the day. What would happen to your friendship with God if you intentionally cultivated an awareness of his presence throughout your day?

The best way to do this is to spend a little time in solitude with God—to remind yourself what it feels like just to be aware of his presence. If you do this in a place without a lot of distractions, you can carry that presence with you throughout your day.

🌱 TODAY'S CHALLENGE

Today, try to practice the presence of God. Be aware that God is everywhere, including wherever you are.

A great way to start is to spend a little time in solitude. If weather permits, find a spot in nature (a beach, forest, park, or your backyard). Be still for at least half an hour, listening to birds, looking at trees and plants, smelling the smells of life. If the weather is inclement, sit by a window that overlooks a garden or some trees. Without praying directly, have an attitude of thankfulness toward God. Enjoy his presence.

If you need something to focus on, pick one of the verses you memorized earlier in this book (see Day Three or Twenty) and reflect on it. Or simply scroll through a mental list of the people you are grateful for and the blessings God has brought to your life, and thank him specifically for each of these people or opportunities.

After your time of being with God, go about your day. Try to keep God in mind; try to be aware of the fact that he is right beside you no matter where you are. If you find you are distracted or forget about him, don't beat yourself up about it. Turn your thoughts toward him once again.

At the end of the day, thank God for his presence in your life. Go to sleep knowing that he will be present and watching over you even as you sleep. Pray that when you wake up, your first thoughts will be of him.

____ *Check here when you have completed today's God Challenge.*

Notes

Father Love

To address God as Abba is the boldest and simplest expression of that absolute trust with which we rely on God for all good, with which we entrust ourselves to him.[64]

—BRENNAN MANNING

When Jesus' disciples asked him how to pray, he told them to follow his example, and to call God "Father." In some prayers, Jesus refers to God as *Abba,* the Aramaic equivalent of *Papa* or *Daddy,* a term of innocent endearment and trust.

For some of us, the metaphor of a Father—someone bigger than us who protects, provides, and loves—is helpful when thinking of God. But for others, the name *Father* has negative connotations. For example, in his book *Crazy Love,* Pastor Francis Chan writes that he felt unwanted and unloved by his father:

I never carried on a meaningful conversation with my dad. In fact, the only affection I remember came when I was nine years old: He put his arm around me for about thirty seconds while we were on our way to my stepmother's funeral. Besides that, the only other physical touch I experienced were the beatings I received when I disobeyed or bothered him.[65]

Not surprisingly, Chan says his strongest feeling toward God when he first became a believer was one of fear.

Most of us got a mixed bag from our earthly fathers: love yet betrayal; kindness yet impatience; goodness yet anger. My own father loved me, but he was distant. First of all, I was the youngest of his eight kids, and he was fifty-eight when I was born. He was a man from another era, an old-school sort of guy who had literally been raised in the woods, where his father ran a sawmill. A World War II Navy vet, he worked hard his whole life. He felt his role was to work and provide, not coddle or offer a lot of affection. I didn't feel terribly close to him, but I don't think he was emotionally close to anyone. My dad did like to talk to me sometimes, and I do know that he loved me, but his life was focused on his work. He'd work all day as a machinist, come home, take off his coveralls and wash up, eat supper, then head out to his workshop to do more work.

Then he retired. Without the work that had defined his life, he became depressed. He ended up waking me up early one morning to say good-bye, then walking outside and taking his own life. I was twelve at the time. For years that influenced my ability to love and trust anyone, including God. The anger and sadness I felt over my dad's death left me scarred. I'm not sure I fully came to grips with it until I became a father myself.

In Chan's book, he also says that becoming a father changed his view of God as a father, because he realized that the love he felt for his little girl was but a fraction of the love God felt for him. Likewise, realizing how much I love my three kids has given me fresh insight into what it means for God to be a father to us. But I had to make some choices to do things differently than my dad. I had to make the hard decision to break the pattern and get emotionally close to them.

When my son Colin was about two years old, I remember him putting on a record and doing a little "happy dance" around the living room. "Papa, dance with me!" he said. My own father, given that invitation, would rather have died than danced with a two-year-old. In that moment, I realized that I had to make a choice. Even though it felt awkward and silly, I decided to be a different sort of dad than my own father had been. So I danced in the living room with my son. It sounds strange to say it, but in many ways that was a turning point for me as a father. It made me aware of the great lengths God is willing to go to show me, his child, the love he has for me.

Today's Challenge

None of us had perfect fathers, and none of us *are* perfect fathers (or mothers). We make mistakes, we love imperfectly, we try and we fail. But today, think about the things you appreciate or respect about your dad—or a person who was a father figure to you, if your dad was absent. Take some time to thank God for your dad and for things you learned from him—even if you had to learn some of those things the hard way.

The only perfect parent is our heavenly Father. God is kind but not over-indulging, gentle but strong, loving without conditions. For today's challenge, make a list of what kind of a Father God is. What characteristics does he exhibit?

Then take a look at the list and pray your way through it. Thank God for the specific ways he has been a loving provider and Father for you. Thank your heavenly Father for loving you, and tell him specifically that you love him.

If you have kids, think about the kind of mom or dad you want to be. It is one thing to hope to be a good parent, but actually being one requires that we make choices about our behavior, our words, and our attitudes. If you want to do things differently than your dad, what are some choices you've made that reflect that desire? What are some choices you need to make? Maybe you need to decide to dance with your two-year-old, or hug your son and say, "I love you," or just listen to your daughter talk about her day. Decide what you can do to be a great parent or a great influencer today.

____ *Check here when you have completed today's God Challenge.*

Notes

Day Thirty-three

Listening Prayer

People are meant to live in an ongoing conversation with God, speaking and being spoken to.[66]

—DALLAS WILLARD

Have you ever been reading your Bible when a verse that applied directly to your situation seemed to jump off the page?

Have you ever prayed about a specific question or problem, only to have a friend offer the perfect insight or advice to address that issue?

Are you attuned to God's presence in your life enough that you can both speak to and listen to him throughout your day?

If not, maybe you haven't been paying attention. God speaks to us through his Word, through other people, and sometimes, by whispering to our souls—bringing thoughts of reassurance, love, or direction to our minds.

As you have worked your way through this book, you've been drawing closer to God. Hopefully the challenges are connecting you more deeply with God, not just during the time you spend doing the challenge, but throughout the rest of your day. Adding a spiritual activity to the day won't help us grow nearly as much as cultivating an ongoing connection with God that we carry with us all the time.

The question is *Do we believe God wants to speak to us?* Do we value his wisdom and presence enough to be always seeking it? And then, are we listening? Are we paying attention to his leadings? Are we reading the Bible expecting not only truth for all mankind but truth that applies to our lives personally?

Walter Wangerin writes that prayer is composed of four intertwined components: We speak, God listens; God speaks, we listen. Without all four activities going on (sometimes simultaneously), he argues that our communication with God is incomplete: "How much love God lavishes on each particular heart when he murmurs words intended for that heart alone! How much love the lonely heart misses if it will not hear the personal word." [67]

When you pray, do you take time to listen for God's word to you?

God is limitless, infinite. So it makes sense that he would be able to reveal himself in an infinite number of ways. If God seems distant, it may not be his fault—maybe you are not paying attention. Do you really notice the beauty of God's creation around you? Do you ignore people who you think aren't that important—and perhaps miss some insight God is offering you through their words?

Rather than try to get God to talk to us, or focus on getting to hear him, we should focus on loving him and receiving his love. We should focus on our personal connection with him.

In Dallas Willard's book *Hearing God,* he writes,

Our failure to hear God has its deepest roots in a failure to understand, accept and grow into a conversational relationship with God, the sort of relationship suited to friends who are mature personalities in a shared enterprise, no matter how different they may be in other respects. It is within such a relationship that our Lord surely intends us to have and to recognize his voice speaking in our hearts as occasion demands.[68]

🌳 TODAY'S CHALLENGE

As we mentioned in Day Three, it is much easier for God to bring Scripture to your conscious mind if you have hidden it in your heart by memorizing. If you read your Bible consistently, God's voice will be familiar to you—you'll be able to discern whether the thoughts that come to your mind are consistent with his character and his will.

Willard adds,

> So our union with God—his presence with us, in which our aloneness is banished and the meaning and full purpose of human existence is realized—*consists chiefly in a conversational relationship with God while we are each consistently and deeply engaged as his friend and co-laborer in the affairs of the kingdom of the heavens.*[69]

Pray that God would reveal himself to you in some way today; that you would grow in that "conversational relationship." Start your day by praying about whatever concerns you. Then, be quiet. You may want to pray, "Speak, Lord, for your servant is listening" (see 1 Samuel 3).

Ask God to speak to you through a Scripture you hadn't noticed before, through the words of a friend, or even in your thoughts. Go through your day with a sense of expectancy that

God will speak. Be conscious of ways God may be trying to communicate with you.

Keep in mind that God does not contradict himself. He speaks with the voice of love, because as the Bible says, God *is* love. Even when he is convicting us about our sinful behavior, he does so in a loving way, without shaming or blaming. God will never tell you to do something that contradicts his Word in Scripture, or something that would hurt you or another person.

Remember that God does want to speak to you, not to boss you around, but because he loves you. He wants to have a conversational friendship with you, in which both of you speak, and both of you listen. Have that conversation today.

_____ *Check here when you have completed today's God Challenge.*

Notes

DAY THIRTY-FOUR

Creation Care

Consider how the wild flowers grow. They do not labor or
spin. Yet I tell you, not even Solomon in all his splendor was
dressed like one of these. If that is how God clothes the grass of
the field, which is here today, and tomorrow is thrown into the
fire, how much more will he clothe you—you of little faith!

—JESUS, LUKE 12:27–28 (NIV 2010)

The Bible says that when God first made people, he put them
in a garden and told them to tend it. He gave them everything
they needed, but, as you know, they messed it up.

Even though we are no longer in Eden, our planet is a marvel, a
place of amazing beauty. God didn't have to make mountains, wa-
terfalls, and rolling hills. He could have made the world all brown
and gray, but instead he made it burst with color and texture and
beauty. Its delicate balance reminds us of God's care for us.

Our planet is also an astronomical miracle. The earth is exactly the right distance from the sun to sustain life. In fact, scientists call this "the Goldilocks theory." Just as the little girl in the

children's story *Goldilocks and the Three Bears* found she preferred a chair, porridge, and a bed that were "just right," scientists say that the earth is at just the right distance from the sun to sustain life. Any farther, and our oceans would freeze. Any closer, and they'd become so hot they would evaporate. The water that is the basis for all living things can remain liquid on our planet because of its distance from the sun.

When you compare Earth to its two closest planetary neighbors, Mars and Venus, you see what would happen if we were in a different location. Venus is too hot (because it is closer to the sun), which causes any water on its surface to evaporate. Mars is too cold, so water freezes. Its atmosphere is too thin.[70]

Natural phenomena that seem like disasters to us, like hurricanes and volcanic eruptions, actually regulate the temperature and atmosphere to keep us in that "just right" balance. *Our planet is a gift.* Beyond its perfect conditions to sustain life, God made it beautiful. The Bible says all created things, including the earth itself, speak of the glory of God just by their existence. (See Psalm 19:1.)

When you look at the stunning variety of bugs, birds, animals, and plants, you see how creative God is. The planet spins on its axis, giving us times of darkness and light that match our natural body rhythms and need for sleep in order to function. Water evaporates, forms clouds, and then nourishes the earth through rain. We're able to grow food on the earth's surface—it's all quite miraculous, if you ponder it.

Like all of God's gifts, our planet must be stewarded wisely. Christians of many backgrounds have a growing concern for creation care. God has created a beautiful place for us to live. Imagine that a friend invites you to his home. You come in, track mud all over the carpet, throw garbage on the floor, and spill soda on the couch without offering to clean it up. We of course wouldn't do that in our own homes, let alone in the home of someone who has invited us as a guest.

This world is our home, but the owner, ultimately, is God. *We are his stewards and his guests, and he has asked us to care for the earth.* We wouldn't intentionally spill stuff on the couch, and we shouldn't pour oil into the ocean either. But that's exactly what human beings are doing. If we truly appreciate the beauty of God's creation, we ought to take care of it.

Small actions make a big difference. When my family started recycling our paper, plastic, cans, and bottles, I was surprised to see how little trash we had left. I felt good knowing that I was adding a lot less to the burgeoning landfills with a minimum of effort. Doing things like walking or biking instead of driving for short trips and picking up trash can be ways of caring for the gift God's given us in the earth.

While we can all take steps to be more "green," we won't be motivated to care for creation unless we first spend some time really noticing the wonder of creation.

❧ Today's Challenge

Today, take some time to get outside. No matter the season, notice the beauty of the trees. Whether their branches are frosted with snow or lush with green leaves, thank God for the trees—they clean the atmosphere and provide oxygen for us to breathe. Look for flowers, bugs, animals, and birds. Think about how God provides for them, and thank him for the beauty of creation. As Jesus said, consider the lilies—spend some time actually *considering* them, that is, reflecting on how God provides for the natural world.

Next, spend a little time doing something that will improve some small part of God's world. Here are some suggestions, but be creative and notice the needs around you:

Many municipalities offer groups the opportunity to adopt a section of public highway to keep it free of litter. Find out how you can get involved with that kind of program. Or, clear away trash and weeds to clean up a vacant lot in your neighborhood.

Perhaps you've noticed that your church yard could use some sprucing up—offer to plant some flowers, trim some bushes, or help with other landscaping work. Or volunteer to mow the lawn of an elderly or disabled neighbor (or perhaps a single mom) whose lawn is getting overgrown.

If you don't already do so, start recycling. If you already recycle, think about ways you could further reduce waste and lessen your impact on the environment: maybe riding your bike instead of driving, unplugging appliances when they're not in use, changing to more energy-efficient light bulbs, or composting. Be creative as you care for creation.

_____ *Check here when you have completed today's God Challenge.*

Notes

Prayer Warriors

*Any concern too small to be turned into a prayer
is too small to be made into a burden.*

—CORRIE TEN BOOM

Exodus 17 tells the story of the first of Israel's many battles in their journey to become a nation. Even before they got to the land God had promised them, the text tells us that "the Amalekites came and attacked the Israelites at Rephidim" (v. 8). From the context we know this happened in the second month after they had left Egypt. They'd barely gotten away from Pharaoh, and already other armies attacked them.

The Amalekites were a strong army of fierce warriors, and the Israelites were—well, let's just assume that as they wandered through the desert, they weren't practicing military maneuvers. They had a great military leader in Joshua, but it quickly became clear to Joshua and Moses that they probably wouldn't win the battle, so they decided to pray.

Moses, along with priests Aaron and Hur, went up on a hill to watch the battle, and to pray like crazy that the Israelites wouldn't get completely slaughtered. Moses lifted his hands in prayer, pleading with God to help in this lopsided contest. And miraculously, God responded—as long as Moses kept praying. When he dropped his hands (and stopped praying), the battle turned against Israel.

Thankfully, Moses had friends with him. They found him a stone to sit on, then they came alongside him and prayed with him, holding up his arms physically—and the implication is supporting him spiritually as well. Moses stood firm, praying with his arms raised, and the fierce Amalekites were defeated by a ragtag group of runaway slaves.

That's an amazing picture of the role friends play in supporting each other. Instead of one man praying alone, we have three people. The two support the one, so that he can pray for all of them. I have to imagine that Aaron and Hur, as they held up Moses' arms, were also praying for the battle, for Moses, and for their own strength not to give out.

Facing life's challenges is always easier with a friend who's got your back. I'm glad that I have friends who will pray *for* me, but even more, I appreciate closer friends who will pray *with* me. Friends who will hold up my arms when I am weary, who remind me not to give up.

I have a close friend, Mike, who is what I call a "two in the morning" friend. If I needed something at two in the morning, I know I could call Mike, and he'd come over. (It's happened.) He and I can talk openly. We pray for each other. We pray *with* each other. Having a Christian friend like that has made my spiritual walk stronger.

Do you have a friend with whom you can talk honestly? Someone you trust? Someone you can actually talk with about something deeper than work, sports, the last movie you saw, or your hectic schedule? Someone you know would help you out, whom you could call when you really needed it? What would happen if you took a risk and invited that person to get together to pray with you?

It's rare to drift into a close friendship. *It requires the guts to initiate taking an existing friendship to a deeper level.* One way to do this is to offer to pray with your friend.

To pray with another person is an important spiritual discipline that will help you grow and experience the presence of God. After all, Jesus said that if two or three are gathered together in his name, he's right there among them (see Matthew 18:20).

The fact is, Jesus often prayed with his friends—the disciples. They paid close attention to what he said, even recording some of his prayers in Scripture (see John 17). Can you imagine sitting among the disciples and praying with Jesus? What a great time of friendship and prayer!

Adele Calhoun writes, "If praying with others helps you concentrate and be consistent in prayer, then prayer partnerships can be a wonderful way of encountering God and offering your concerns to him."[71]

A prayer partner can encourage you and hold you accountable. When you're feeling discouraged or disconnected from God, having someone to pray with can pull you back on track. A prayer partner also keeps you from being too self-absorbed— after all, you are not praying only for yourself but for the other person as well. For some of us, that's an important spiritual discipline in itself—to be concerned about the interests of others, not just our own (see Philippians 2).

🌱 TODAY'S CHALLENGE

Who is someone you consider a spiritual friend? If you're already in a small group, can you think of someone from the group who might have the potential to be a closer friend?

Invite this person to pray with you. You could simply send an e-mail, or call and tell them you are trying to grow spiritually, and you'd like to try praying together. Or, tell them about this book.

When you pray, spend time not only on your requests, but on praising God together, thanking him for blessings or answered prayer, and, if the friendship is strong enough, confessing to each other and to God.

It may be easier to structure your time together by using a list of specific things to pray about. If that's the case, before you pray, write down the following for each of you:

- the people in each person's family and what they need prayer for
- each person's personal requests
- the people you both know who are going through a hard time, physically or emotionally or financially
- the things you are thankful for
- the people you both know who need God and don't yet know him

Consider making this a regular practice, even if you have to pray together over the phone. You'll find that having a prayer partner will help you to grow closer to God, and closer to each other.

_____ *Check here when you have completed today's God Challenge.*

Notes

Deciding to Grow

Obedience has a way of strengthening rather than depleting our resources. If we obey in one small corner, we will have power to obey elsewhere. Obedience begets obedience.[72]

—RICHARD FOSTER

The spiritual life is a journey. The goal is to become more like Jesus, to live as he would if he were in our place. The goal is not to avoid ever making a mistake, but to keep moving forward, to make the journey one of wonder and discovery. The goal, in a way, is to never get bored with God—to keep discovering more about him as you are trying to be more like him.

To begin the journey really isn't so tough. As the old hymn says, Jesus will accept us just as we are. The true test is endurance—*will we continue to believe, and will we also continue to grow?* Hebrews 12:1 exhorts us, "Let us throw off everything that hinders and the sin that so easily entangles, and let us run with perseverance the race marked out for us."

Will we run the race marked out for us? Will the journey take us to new places, or back to the same old routine? That choice is entirely up to us.

Dallas Willard makes a helpful distinction between intention and decision. For example, suppose you intend to have abs of steel. You may deeply desire to be fit and strong. So you buy an exercise video that you saw on a late-night infomercial. That's a decision. But it must be followed by other decisions. The next day, you put the DVD in and sit down on the couch and watch every minute. After a week, will you be transformed? How about after a month?

Of course, the example is ridiculous. You can't get in shape by sitting on the couch watching a workout video (unfortunately). Until you actually decide to get off the couch, until you begin doing the exercises, until you put down the snacks and pick up the barbell, you won't get in shape, no matter how earnestly you intend to do so. You must decide, and that decision must result in action. Decisions, acted upon, lead to transformation.

Spiritually, the same is true. We must decide to obey God, and then actually do it. Intending to follow him won't cut it. You might want to grow; you might deeply desire to be closer to God, to live like Jesus. But thinking about it isn't enough. You've got to decide, and then carry out those decisions. Just reading this book, for example, without doing the challenges is like sitting on the couch watching an exercise video and hoping it will build your biceps.

Have you decided to grow? If you think you haven't made a decision about it either way, you are fooling yourself. The lack of a decision to grow is a decision to stay stuck.

When I was about forty years old, I was working as a literary agent and had the privilege of representing Brennan Manning, author of *The Ragamuffin Gospel* and several other books. I deeply respect Brennan because he's an amazing writer. But more than that, I respect his spiritual life. He seems to have an authentic connection with God that I deeply admire.

I remember a conversation with Brennan describing what I felt was going on with me spiritually, seeking his wisdom and advice. I was surprised when he told me: "Most men, if you look at where they are spiritually when they're in the mid-forties, have pretty much decided that's where they will be for the rest of their lives. They really don't grow or change much after that." That conversation had a profound effect on me. He said I had already peaked spiritually. Seriously? I was essentially done growing? I thought it was interesting that Brennan said most guys *decided* this—because I think it is perhaps an unconscious decision.

But over time I realized he was right and also that this truth applies to women as well as men. By the time you're in your forties, you've pretty much decided what role you'll have in church, how involved you'll be, and what sort of spiritual impact you'll have on others. New ministries within the church are generally started by younger women and men. It's pretty rare to take a huge spiritual leap in your fifties, or to suddenly become deacon or elder material in your sixties.

I determined that day that I wasn't going to be the same person, spiritually speaking, at fifty that I had been at forty. I wanted to continue the journey, to continue to get closer to God, to be a more loving, kind, patient, and gentle guy. For that to happen, I had to not only wish it to be so, I had to make daily decisions to follow God, to pray, to engage in spiritual disciplines, to be in a small group, to choose to love and serve my family.

Of course, I make mistakes. Like everyone else, I mess up, get impatient, and act unkind. I've sometimes made bad decisions.

I am known to be a bit sarcastic, and when my humor goes too far, I hurt people's feelings. I try to own it and apologize, but it happens. I lean heavily into God's grace, because I am a sinner like everyone else. But I think I have made progress on the journey, and am continuing to do so at age fifty-two. I am closer to God now than I was at forty, in part because of God's grace, because of that conversation with Brennan, but also because I made that decision.

In my view, my spiritual growth came down to choices: Would I decide to keep on following Jesus and continue to grow in my spiritual journey, or would I decide to coast?

🌱 Today's Challenge

The spiritual practices and disciplines you've tried as you've read this book provided you with the opportunity to experiment, to try doing something to improve your relationship with God. The question becomes, which of these will you continue to practice once you're done reading this book? Which of the various practices seemed to bring you into God's presence or help you experience his love? Which ones challenged you to grow?

As you are nearing the end of this forty-day adventure, you must decide whether you will continue to practice some of the disciplines you've learned. You've got to decide if you are going to pray, study, fast, memorize, and serve. You have to choose between pride and humility, between your way and God's way.

Today, make a list of some of the practices you would like to continue to do and how often you intend to do them. Which practices will help you on your journey? You won't do everything every day. But how often *will* you do them? Perhaps some things, like prayer, will be daily practices. Others, like memorization or solitude or fasting, might be weekly or monthly practices. Start slowly and build as you continue the journey. Take a few minutes to figure out what practices you'd like to make a part of your everyday life.

____ *Check here when you have completed today's God Challenge.*

Notes

DAY THIRTY-SEVEN

Humility

What comes into our minds when we think about God is the most important thing about us.[73]

—A. W. TOZER

What do you think about God? Is he there only to help you? Is he disappointing you, or demanding too much of you? Or are you in awe of him, amazed by him? Or do you not think about him very much at all?

One of the dangers of undertaking the challenge of trying to grow spiritually is that we can begin to focus more on ourselves and less on God. As we add spiritual practices to our routine, as we see forward movement on our journey toward him, we can be tempted to self-focus, to pat ourselves on the back because we are becoming so deep, or to take pride in our newfound maturity. Pride is an ever-present temptation, especially when things are going well in our relationship with God.

But the point of this book, or any other spiritual endeavor, is that we would increasingly be focused on God, not on ourselves. As we grow, God should be more and more the focus of our lives. He should become, in a way, *a larger presence in our lives.*

C. S. Lewis's *Prince Caspian,* the second book in the *Chronicles of Narnia,* contains a wonderful scene where Lucy encounters Aslan the lion (the Christ figure in the stories) for the first time in quite a while. She notices that he has gotten bigger since the last time she's seen him.

> "That is because you are older, little one," answered he.
>> "Not because you are?"
> "I am not. But every year you grow, you will find me bigger." [74]

What a beautiful way to draw a picture of the goal of our spiritual life. It echoes John the Baptist's sentiment, "He must increase, but I must decrease" (John 3:30 KJV).

Philippians 2:3–4 says: "Do nothing out of selfish ambition or vain conceit, but in humility consider others better than yourselves. Each of you should look not only to your own interests, but also to the interests of others."

But what does that mean? And how can we be humble without becoming proud of how humble we are?

Adele Calhoun notes:

> Humility does not mean thinking demeaning and low thoughts about ourselves. It's not denying the truth of our achievements or thinking less of ourselves. Humility stems from an honest understanding of who we are. . . . Humility stems from having someone besides yourself as the center of your attention. [75]

Calhoun suggests such practical steps as "refusing the impulse to name-drop" or "deliberately keeping silent about accomplishments" as steps toward humility.

Humility is a spiritual discipline, one necessary to combat the sin of pride. *It's built through serving others, but also by spending time reflecting on the greatness of God, his power and strength and wisdom, and how that exceeds our own.* Humble people have a right-sized view of themselves, and a right-sized view of God. He is not just a bigger version of us, he's beyond anything we can imagine; he is infinite in power and strength and goodness. We cannot comprehend him fully.

I hate talking about this topic since, frankly, I can struggle with being an arrogant jerk. I often feel like my humility is all false—that what I really want is to tell everyone how great I am. But I don't *want* to be a jerk. My desire is to demonstrate humility, and to treat others like Jesus. I think too many people confuse humility with a lack of confidence. But it takes great inner strength to be humble. You can be humble and confident at the same time—Christ was. But your confidence will not be in yourself—it will be in God. The key to true humility, then, is to look at God rather than at ourselves.

🌿 TODAY'S CHALLENGE

Read Job 38–41. This passage is God's response to Job's question, "Why me?" as he struggles with the pain and suffering he's had to endure in this life. (If you have never read the book of Job, you may want to read the whole book, just to get the context of God's words in these chapters.)

God reminds Job that he is small, that there's much he doesn't understand. As you read, imagine God is saying these words to you. What thoughts or questions come to mind? What situations have you experienced where you thought too highly of yourself, or questioned God, or came across as arrogant?

Countless sermons have been preached on the meaning of this passage, as well as on the book of Job itself. I really like Mark

Buchanan's take on this passage, which is a bit different from the typical interpretation. He comments:

> Maybe God's not taunting or scolding Job at all, or at least not just this. Instead, or perhaps as well, God is wooing him. He's dazzling him. He's answering his misery and agony and boredom with a call to fresh wonder, trying to make Job childlike again. He's saying, in effect, *Look, Job! Look at what I've made! You have been sitting on this dung pile so long, with this pain in your heart and in your flesh so long, with these boring windbags haranguing you for so long, that you've grown blind to beauty. Everyone's trying to fix you, Job, fix your problem. Not Me. I'm going to wow you. I'm going to put fire back in your belly.*[76]

Think about your finiteness and God's infinite power and knowledge. Be still before him—not in shame but in reverence. And then remind yourself that you should be humble not only because there is so much you don't know, but because there is so much God knows. He is amazing and worthy of our praise and admiration.

Spend some time worshiping God for who he is. Thank him for loving you despite the fact that you could never do anything to earn his love or favor. Express your amazement and wonder at God's power and knowledge and strength.

____ *Check here when you have completed today's God Challenge.*

Notes

Celebrate

*Freedom from anxiety and care forms the basis
for celebration. . . . Celebration brings joy into
life, and joy makes us strong.*[77]

—RICHARD FOSTER

When my kids were small, my wife and I would occasionally put them to bed a little early. We'd wait a few minutes for them to settle down, then we'd burst into their rooms yelling, "Pajama ride! Pajama ride!" We'd herd them out to the car, still in their pajamas, and drive to Dairy Queen, where we'd all enjoy ice cream.

Why? Absolutely no reason—except that it was fun and the kids loved it. We enjoyed seeing how delighted they became at just taking the time to do something fun and silly. Of course they loved eating ice cream, but the novelty of going to DQ in your pajamas never got old. Now that I'm a grandfather, I'm hoping my son will occasionally take my granddaughter on pajama rides. (Or maybe I'll do it. Since she's not yet a year old, I guess we've got plenty of time for pajama rides.)

I've long believed one of God's greatest gifts is that of laughter. Yet it is often a gift we leave untouched, or else we think it is something that has absolutely no connection to our spiritual lives. (I once heard a popular preacher make the point that the Bible never records Jesus laughing. But who wants a Father with no sense of fun? Who wants to believe Jesus never enjoyed himself?) Laughter can heal us, and joy can give us supernatural strength.

How often do you laugh? How often do you celebrate? Joy is among the characteristics that God's Spirit is cultivating in our lives (see Galatians 5:22). What are you doing in your life to cooperate with the Spirit's efforts to make you more joyful?

I'm a very goal-oriented person. I set goals, work hard, and get things done. One of the things I sometimes forget to do is to *celebrate those accomplishments.* I'm not talking about being self-absorbed or trying to call attention to myself. But it's a good idea to stop every once in a while and notice the blessings of God in my life. I want to stop, remember the things he's given me, and celebrate a goal achieved. I want to actually enjoy my success rather than immediately pressing on to the next project.

Beyond celebrating specific things, we ought to celebrate at times for no reason at all, simply because we can. It may seem an odd thing to you, but throughout the Old Testament God commands his people to celebrate. Festivals, feasts, and celebrations were to be a part of the rhythm of life for God's people. He would tell them to stop their work, get some good food and wine, and have a feast. (See, for example, Deuteronomy 14:22–27.)

Maybe there's a history of believers not enjoying life enough, since God had to command people to have a party. But if you really think about it, how often do you celebrate? And when you do have a party, is it to acknowledge and celebrate the good things God has done, or is it merely a means of escaping your stress? I understand we all live in a lost and broken world. You have problems—so do I. We often grind through life, without stopping to notice what

God has done or celebrating what he's helped us to accomplish. Too often we don't stop to celebrate and express our gratitude. That's why God had to command his people to do so.

God told people in Scripture to celebrate the harvest whether it was big or small, and to remember His deliverance on Passover even while they were in captivity and exile. Celebration is a discipline. Deciding to be joyful and to celebrate can actually change our attitude.

Sometimes we have to choose to focus on the positive. Did you know that simply smiling, whether you feel like it or not, can lift your mood? I'm not recommending pretending everything's great when you are in the midst of struggle. Sometimes life is painful. But even in those seasons, we can look for the good things. We can choose to celebrate and be joyful, in spite of our struggles. The Bible says:

> A cheerful heart is a good medicine,
>   but a downcast spirit dries up the bones.
>
> Proverbs 17:22 NRSV

So at times we have to choose to laugh. We have to decide to be cheerful and upbeat.

Nehemiah 8:10 says, "The joy of the Lord is your strength." Joy and laughter heal us and strengthen us. We're free to find many ways to celebrate—with feasts as the Bible often recommends, with worship and singing, and even with laughing among friends.

🌳 Today's Challenge

Today, be intentional about laughter, joy, and celebration. Take time to celebrate accomplishments, or to have fun for no reason.

If you have children, take them on a pajama ride or some other spontaneous, fun outing. Find the strength that comes to your soul when you decide to be joyful.

As you go through your day, smile. If you have kids and they are being silly, don't reprimand them. Laugh along with them.

Look for an opportunity to laugh. Be intentional about this—if you need help, take some time to read comics online (maybe *Dilbert* or *The Far Side*), watch an old favorite comedy movie, or read a funny book or essay. Call a friend who always makes you laugh. And as you laugh, thank God for providing humor and joy in our lives.

"Poke fun at yourself," recommends Richard Foster. "Enjoy wholesome jokes and clever puns. Relish good comedy. Learn to laugh; it is a discipline to be mastered. Let go the everlasting burden of always needing to sound profound."[78]

Today, find a reason to celebrate, and do it. Plan a party: invite some friends over, serve a great meal (or order a pizza), and take some time to name the blessings in your life.

____ *Check here when you have completed today's God Challenge.*

Notes

Day Thirty-nine

Family Ties

When we pray for our children, we are asking God to
make His presence a part of their lives and work power-
fully in their behalf. [79]

—Stormie Omartian

I pray as a spiritual discipline, as a means to building my relationship with God. Still, I wouldn't call myself a "prayer warrior." It
doesn't always come easy to me. I often think I ought to pray
more. Sometimes I neglect prayer—although I soon realize that
God feels distant, and I need to draw near to him again.

While my motivation for prayer in general sometimes wavers,
my motivation for prayer for my family is much stronger. I've
got three kids, a daughter-in-law, and a granddaughter—all of
whom put up with me, which isn't easy. I love to pray for them.
One of my girls spends her time living in developing countries,
so it's easy to pray for her safety. I have a granddaughter, Maelie,
whom I enjoy seeing grow and change. Praying for those closest
to me is fairly easy.

If you have children, do you pray for them? If you are married, do you pray for your spouse? Sometimes we're more motivated to pray when our spouse or kids are doing things we don't like— we pray they will change. But intercessory prayer is not about manipulating or trying to control; it's about asking God that his will be done in the lives of the people we love.

Parents with a child in a "prodigal" season, or people in a difficult marriage, may find themselves praying for those circumstances to be changed or resolved. But I've often found that God wants to change my attitude, to get me to trust him, and to work in the lives of my family members to teach them something or draw them to him. He asks me to trust.

A few years ago, my son graduated college and got married in the same season. Not long after, both our daughters took off for overseas study programs in Europe.

My wife and I found ourselves suddenly looking around, surprised at how empty our nest had become. I missed my kids terribly, but I found that as they embarked on these adventures I was more motivated than ever to pray for them.

Of course I've always prayed for my kids—anyone who has raised kids through their teen years knows what I'm talking about. But in recent years, as my son has become a father, as my daughters have continued their education and begun focusing on their careers, I find myself praying for them a lot more. It feels like there is so much at stake. And they're out of my house, so I don't have as much input in their lives.

We've talked in previous chapters about prayer, and it's often been focused on prayer for yourself, or prayer that will deepen your individual relationship with God. But prayer is a gift we can give others. The Bible tells us to intercede for one another.

Jesus prayed for his disciples, and we are to pray for each other. A great place to start is to pray for our families.

If you are not married or don't have kids, you can pray for your parents, siblings, or extended family members. Maybe you have a grandparent or parent who is older and facing health issues, or a sibling who is struggling in some way. Maybe there is a rift in a relationship with someone in your family, and you need to pray for healing between you and that person.

Look, none of us has a perfect family. Most of us experienced both joy and pain in the family we grew up in. As I've told you in previous chapters, I was deeply wounded by my father's suicide, as were my siblings. However, I also received some good things from my dad—my love of reading, for example, and my strong work ethic. Even if you were hurt by your family, or abandoned by them, you can still pray for them.

God fills in the gaps in our upbringing so that we can love our family better. That means we are able to give things we never got from our earthly fathers. Part of maturing is learning to understand and honor your parents, even if you don't agree with everything they did or do. And often prayer moves us far along the path to this maturity. When we pray for people, it changes our relationship with them. If your relationship with your parents, siblings, or extended family is marked by tension and strife, it may seem hard to fix. And you cannot fix it yourself. *But you can pray for them.*

Realizing that I am deeply loved by a perfect God who will never leave me or forsake me enables me to love others in a whole new way. It enables me to love my family, to choose to be a better dad than my dad was, and to realize I need to offer grace to others because I've been offered incredible grace from God. And one way to become a better father and husband is by praying for my family.

 # Today's Challenge

In her book *The Power of a Praying Parent,* Stormie Omartian writes that prayer is not a way to manipulate your kids, but a way to invite God's power into their lives:

> Prayer is acknowledging and experiencing the presence of God and inviting His presence into our lives and circumstances. It's seeking the *presence* of God and recognizing the *power* of God which gives us the means to overcome any problem.[80]

Today, pray for your family members—your spouse, if you're married; your children, if you have them; your siblings, parents, or extended family. In addition to praying for whatever challenges each of your family members is facing, pray for their spiritual lives. Pray that they would grow, that they would draw closer to God, that they would see his purpose in the midst of whatever they might be going through. Pray for strength, comfort, and growth. Tell God you love them, and you know he loves them too.

____ *Check here when you have completed today's God Challenge.*

Notes

Day Forty

Finish Strong

*Mere change is not growth. Growth is the synthesis of
change and continuity, and where there is no continuity
there is no growth.*[81]

—C. S. Lewis

When you take a child in for his annual checkup, the doctor will
always measure his height and weight. Why? Because he wants
to make sure he is growing. Growth is a sign of health. We may
vaguely notice that little Johnny seems a bit taller or seems to be
outgrowing his clothes, but we're often surprised when he goes
for a checkup to learn that he's grown a few inches in the past year.

In the same way, we may not notice on a daily basis the slow
growth of our spirit—the way we are becoming kinder, more
loving, more patient people. So it's important to stop once in a
while and reflect on how far we've come.

Each of us has to know how to interpret change. If little
Johnny has gained weight but not height, that is not necessarily
healthy, unless he started the year terribly underweight. A doctor

is looking at overall health to make sure the changes in Johnny's size are actually an improvement. As C. S. Lewis points out in the quote above, change is not the only goal—*growth is the goal*. And growth happens in the confluence of both change and continuity. For example, although a child may change physically, if he's healthy, then along with changes like getting taller or bigger there will also be continuity: all his systems will continue to function and thrive. Some changes can often be the sign of poor health—changes in our appetite, the appearance of our skin, changes in our hearing, our vision, and our overall demeanor can be a sign that something is wrong. So change alone is not growth.

The same is true spiritually. To simply change is not the ultimate goal. For Christians, *spiritual growth is about becoming more like Jesus*. Changing our routine to incorporate spiritual disciplines like the ones you've learned in this book is certainly a change. But is it growth? Not necessarily. The disciplines themselves are not growth—they create space in our lives for growth. What's going on inside of us? Is our heart becoming more like the heart of Jesus? Are we experiencing God's love in a more significant way? Are we staying faithful?

In other words, if I have changed, has it been a change for the better? I may be reading my Bible more regularly, but if my inner attitude is one of superiority and pride about that, it cannot be called growth. I may have given up bad habits, but if I have replaced them with inner attitudes of anger or selfishness, I have not grown.

Today is a day to reflect on the change and growth that has occurred in your life recently. First, congratulations—you've made it to the last day of our walk together toward getting closer to God. In the last forty days, you've tried many spiritual practices: prayer, solitude, fasting, study, memorization, giving, self-examination, service, and more.

But as you know, *just checking these things off your list is not the end goal.* Rather, these disciplines are a means to transformative growth. This forty-day challenge was an opportunity for you to learn some things about yourself. Do you love to study more than you thought you did? Were you surprised by anything? Which practices or disciplines were you drawn to? Which did you enjoy most? Which disciplines were more of a stretch for you? Did you feel like you had to force yourself to do some of the practices? Which ones made you feel uncomfortable or resistant?

In addition to having a preference for specific disciplines, we also each have a spiritual temperament, or what Gary Thomas calls a spiritual pathway. We're all wired differently—some of us are activists, others are more contemplative. Some feel closest to God when engaging their mind in study; others feel God's presence most acutely when they are out in the beauty and wildness of creation.

We have a lot of freedom in how we relate to God—but that freedom is not meant to be abused. Hopefully this forty-day challenge has allowed you to experiment with your spiritual life. As you've tried various things, you've hopefully grown closer to God, grown to understand yourself better, and now will be able to have a more positive influence on the people around you.

🌳 TODAY'S CHALLENGE

Spend some time today reading back through the list of various practices you've tried. If you used the space for journaling, take some time to read back over what you've written. Do you see progress from the first day to the last? Think about which activities made a big impression on you. Take some time to write down honestly what you enjoyed and what you would prefer to forget. Look for God's leading as you reflect—what did you learn? How has your focus changed?

Nothing you do can make God love you more (or love you less, for that matter). But growth has a purpose in your life, and in the lives of the people around you. Your spiritual growth will improve your marriage, your parenting, your friendships, the way you relate to co-workers, and even your role in church.

Robert Mulholland writes that "spiritual formation is a process of being conformed to the image of Christ *for the sake of others.* . . . Our relationships with others are not only the testing grounds of our spiritual life but also the places where our growth toward wholeness in Christ happens."[82] Your spiritual growth will not only draw you closer to God, it will help reshape all of your relationships. In fact, it could point others toward God, as you reflect him better in your daily life. Christ wants you to be transformed so that you might be an agent of transformation in the lives of others. I pray this book has helped you take steps toward that.

____ *Check here when you have completed today's God Challenge.*

Notes

Acknowledgments

As I stated earlier, my life has been all about *books* and *people.*

My earliest memories are of books and words, and my life was shaped by the stories of Robert Louis Stevenson and Kenneth Grahame and C. S. Lewis. I loved hearing about *The Scottish Chiefs.* I still read *Treasure Island* occasionally, if only to remember the thrill I got from imagining myself as young Jim Hawkins facing down Long John Silver.

There's no doubt about it—books have changed my life. But no book can replace a person. That's why Christ came himself, instead of just sending us his stories in a cool novel. For all my love of books, it is *people* who have discipled me and shaped my spiritual walk. People have invested in me in some way; they've shared their wisdom, and that has helped change me.

I was only twelve years old when my dad committed suicide, and a young man by the name of Jim Peabody stepped in to help me learn what being a Christian was all about. Jim isn't someone you've heard of—he wasn't famous, he didn't write any books, he won't show up in any history of the church. He pushed a broom at the Oregon Steel Mill, never served as a formal pastor, and wasn't known outside a small group of us in the Portland area. But Jim loved Jesus, discipled a bunch of young men, and through his service the world is a different place. The guys he helped grow spiritually are now businessmen and pastors and leaders and military officers (and literary agents). Through Jim's quiet ministry, lives were indelibly changed.

When I went off to grad school, I met a pastor by the name of Curt Heffelfinger, who gathered a small group of us around him to invest in us and show us what it means to pastor a flock. He's not famous, and never built a mega-church, but he helped a bunch of us figure out how to be leaders and walk closer with God. Two of the guys in the group, Sid Rogers and Sam Rima, formed a small group with me, and we walked one another through classes and training and learning how to be husbands. It was in learning all the steps and putting them into practice that we matured. We were probably immature and awful at the beginning—in fact, I might have been immature and awful at the end, but I'm sure I was further down the path after a few years with those men. And the pastors in my life—Steve Watkins, Frank Lednicky, Steve Hixon, Ken Ross—have all taken the time to build into me. They all mentored me and moved me beyond reading about the faith in order to help me live it out.

When I started writing full-time, longtime freelance writer Steve Halliday not only showed me how to do that job, he actually arranged to have work sent my way so that I wouldn't starve; then he introduced me to people in the Christian publishing industry. John Van Diest also introduced me around to people in the industry and gave me a job as a senior editor.

I probably owe more to Rick Christian than anyone. Rick helped me become an agent and showed me how to be successful. My friend Mike Allison has been a spiritual Barnabas to me throughout my life. And my business partner, Sandra Bishop, has given me as much as I've given her.

My reason for mentioning all these names? Because you need to understand that the book you're holding is the result of a bunch of people who all helped me grow. There's nothing in here that some other person didn't first share with me. Nearly every page quotes a book—my homage to the writers and thinkers I appreciate.

It wouldn't be right to fail to mention Andy McGuire, my editor and the guy who first approached me with this idea. Thanks for coming to me with it first. And finally, I need to thank my collaborator, Keri Wyatt Kent, a great writer and friend who took some of my stories and pushed them all over the top with her skill. Thanks for being more talented than I, Keri.

I love books, but I have grown weary of hearing people tell me they were "discipled by the apostle Paul" or "mentored by Saint John." They weren't. They might have been influenced by the words, but it takes a friend—someone with flesh and blood who can stand in front of you and say, "Let's try this" or "Here's how you do that." For all the mentors who have presented me with my own God challenge, I want to say thanks. I'm not worthy of your work, but I'm trying to move forward.

Notes

1. John Ortberg, *The Life You've Always Wanted* (Grand Rapids, MI: Zondervan, 1997), 108.

2. John Kirvan, *God Hunger* (Notre Dame, IN: Sorin Books, 1999), 12.

3. Marjorie Thompson, *Soul Feast* (Louisville, KY: Westminster John Knox Press, 1995), 69–71.

4. Ibid., 71.

5. Ortberg, *The Life You've Always Wanted*, 186.

6. Walter Wangerin, *Whole Prayer* (Grand Rapids, MI: Zondervan, 1998), 51–52.

7. Henri Nouwen, *The Inner Voice of Love* (New York: Doubleday, 1996), xvi.

8. Rick Warren, *The Purpose-Driven Life* (Grand Rapids, MI: Zondervan, 2004), 222.

9. Philip Yancey, *Soul Survivor* (Colorado Springs: Multnomah, 2003), 261.

10. Adele Calhoun, *Spiritual Disciplines Handbook* (Downers Grove, IL: InterVarsity Press, 2005), 57.

11. Philip Yancey, *What's So Amazing About Grace?* (Grand Rapids, MI: Zondervan, 1997), 45.

12. Francis Chan, *Crazy Love* (Colorado Springs: David C. Cook, 2008), 29.

13. Annie Dillard, *The Writing Life* (New York: Harper & Row, 1989), 32.

14. Calhoun, *Spiritual Disciplines Handbook*, 224.

15. Robert Benson, *In Constant Prayer* (Nashville, TN: Thomas Nelson, 2008), 9.

16. Richard Carlson and Joseph Bailey, *Slowing Down to the Speed of Life* (New York: HarperSanFrancisco, 1997), xxiii.

17. Thomas Kelly, *A Testament of Devotion* (New York: HarperSanFrancisco, [1941], 1992 edition), 69.

18. Anne Lamott, "Time Lost and Found," *Sunset*, April 2010, *www.sunset.com/travel/anne-lamott-how-to-find-time-00418000067331/*.

19. C. S. Lewis, *Letters to Malcolm: Chiefly on Prayer* (New York: Harcourt Brace Jovanovich, 1964), 93.

20. Bill Hybels, *Too Busy Not to Pray* (Downers Grove, IL: InterVarsity Press, 1988), 56.

21. Ortberg, *The Life You've Always Wanted*, 67.

22. Hybels, *Too Busy Not to Pray*, 57.

23. David Benner, *Sacred Companions* (Downers Grove, IL: InterVarsity Press, 2002), 27.

24. Walter Hooper, ed., *The Letters of C. S. Lewis to Arthur Greeves (1914–1963)* (New York: Collier/Macmillan, 1986), 477.

25. Benner, *Sacred Companions*, 70.

26. C. S. Lewis, *The Four Loves* (New York: Harcourt Brace Jovanovich, 1960), 96–97.

27. Don E. Saliers, "Singing Our Lives" in *Practicing Our Faith*, Dorothy Bass, ed. (San Francisco: Jossey-Bass, 1997), 186. Saliers is a United Methodist minister and professor of theology and liturgy as well as director of the Master of Sacred Music program at Emory University's Candler School of Theology.

28. Ibid., 180.

29. Rob Bell, *Velvet Elvis: Repainting the Christian Faith* (Grand Rapids, MI: Zondervan, 2005), 62–63.

30. Stephanie Strom, "Pledge to Give Away Half Gains Billionaire Adherents," *New York Times*, August 4, 2010, *www.nytimes.com/2010/08/05/us/05giving.html*.

31. Philip Yancey, *Prayer: Does It Make Any Difference?* (Grand Rapids, MI: Zondervan, 2006), 172.

32. *Dictionary of the Old Testament Wisdom, Poetry and Writings,* Tremper Longman and Peter Enns, eds. (Downers Grove, IL: InterVarsity Press, 2008), 385.

33. A. W. Tozer, *The Pursuit of God* (Camp Hill, PA: Christian Publications, Inc., 1982).

34. Ortberg, *The Life You've Always Wanted,* 17.

35. Shane Claiborne, *The Irresistible Revolution* (Grand Rapids, MI: Zondervan, 2006), 113.

36. Chan, *Crazy Love,* 93.

37. Tozer, *The Pursuit of God,* 11.

38. Parker Palmer, *A Hidden Wholeness* (San Francisco: Jossey-Bass, 2004), 58–59.

39. Ruth Haley Barton, *Invitation to Solitude and Silence* (Downers Grove, IL: InterVarsity Press, 2004), 31.

40. Quoted in Richard Baxter, *Memoirs of Margaret Baxter* (London: Richard Edwards, 1826), 14.

41. Jonathan Edwards, *The Works of Jonathan Edwards* (William Ball, Paternoster-Row, 1839), 557.

42. From a sermon quoted at *www.csec.org/csec/sermon/smedes_4101.htm.* If this is an issue for you, please read through the whole message and the interview with Smedes on this site. You'll find truth that will set you free.

43. John Piper, *Desiring God* (Colorado Springs: Multnomah, 1996), 19.

44. Rebecca Manley Pippert, *Out of the Saltshaker and Into the World* (Downers Grove, IL: InterVarsity, 1999), 113.

45. Ann Spangler and Lois Tverberg, *Sitting at the Feet of Rabbi Jesus* (Grand Rapids, MI: Zondervan, 2009), 132.

46. Ibid., 141. The authors credit Joachim Jeremias for his insights on this topic. See Joachim Jeremias, *New Testament Theology.*

47. Yancey, *Prayer: Does It Make Any Difference?,* 49.

48. Calhoun, *Spiritual Disciplines Handbook,* 44.

49. Mark Twain, *The Official Web Site of Mark Twain, http://cmgww.com/historic/twain/about/quotes2.htm.*

50. Anne Lamott, *Bird by Bird* (New York: Doubleday, 1994), 100.

51. Dietrich Bonhoeffer, *The Cost of Discipleship* (New York: MacMillan Publishing [1949], 1963 edition), 177.

52. Ibid., 176.

53. Ortberg, *The Life You've Always Wanted*, 111.

54. Ibid.

55. Brennan Manning, *Ruthless Trust* (New York: Harper SanFrancisco, 2000), 3.

56. Richard Foster, *Celebration of Discipline* (New York: Harper & Row, 1988), 145.

57. Calhoun, *Spiritual Disciplines Handbook*, 92–93.

58. Thompson, *Soul Feast*, 90.

59. Foster, *Celebration of Discipline*, 144.

60. Richard Foster, *Freedom of Simplicity* (New York: HarperCollins, 1981), 7.

61. Søren Kierkegaard, *Purity of Heart Is to Will One Thing* (New York: Harper Brothers, 1938).

62. Foster, *Freedom of Simplicity*, 9–10.

63. Lewis, *Letters to Malcolm*, 75.

64. Brennan Manning, *The Wisdom of Tenderness* (New York: HarperSanFrancisco, 2002), 29.

65. Chan, *Crazy Love*, 54.

66. Dallas Willard, *Hearing God* (Downers Grove, IL: InterVarsity Press, 1984), 18.

67. Wangerin, *Whole Prayer*, 35.

68. Willard, *Hearing God*, 29.

69. Ibid., 56.

70. Learn more at *www.windows2universe.org/earth/interior/Goldilocks.html*.

71. Calhoun, *Spiritual Disciplines Handbook*, 243.

72. Richard Foster, *Prayer: Finding the Heart's True Home* (New York: HarperCollins, 1992), 72.

73. A. W. Tozer, *The Knowledge of the Holy* (New York: Harper & Row, 1961), 1.

74. C. S. Lewis, *Prince Caspian* (New York: Macmillan [1951], reissued 1988), 117.

75. Calhoun, *Spiritual Disciplines Handbook,* 191.

76. Mark Buchanan, *The Holy Wild* (Colorado Springs: Multnomah, 2003), 184–185.

77. Foster, *Celebration of Discipline,* 191.

78. Ibid., 198.

79. Stormie Omartian, *The Power of a Praying Parent* (Eugene, OR: Harvest House Publishers, 2007), 20.

80. Ibid., 19.

81. C. S. Lewis, *Selected Literary Essays,* Walter Hooper, ed. (Cambridge: Cambridge University Press, 1979), 105.

82. M. Robert Mulholland Jr., *Invitation to a Journey* (Downers Grove, IL: InterVarsity Press, 1993), 12, 43.

About the Authors

Jerry MacGregor has written more than two dozen titles, including two books that hit #1 on the bestseller lists in their category. Jerry earned his master's degree from Talbot Theological Seminary and did his doctoral work at the University of Oregon. He lives with his wife in Nehalem, Oregon.

Keri Wyatt Kent is the author of eight books and is a regular contributor to *Kyria.com* (formerly *Today's Christian Woman*), *Outreach* magazine, and *Momsense* magazine. Keri speaks at churches and retreats around the country and is a frequent guest on several shows on the Moody Broadcasting Network, including *Midday Connection*. Keri lives with her husband and two children in suburban Chicago.